nections with the IWW that a fair trial became an impossibility. He examines the refusal of the Utah Supreme Court to reverse the conviction, and shows how the Court, in its desire to send an IWW leader to his execution, actually place during

Dr. Foner great defense Hill's behalf,

AFL and the Socialist Party were united. He describes how, through petitions, mass meetings and demonstrations, many thousands of workers in the United States and abroad voiced their protests at the conviction and demanded a new trial. The campaign reached such heights that the Swedish Minister to the United States became actively involved in the movement to save Joe Hill's life, and President Woodrow Wilson twice appealed to the Utah authorities to delay execution. Dr. Foner then relates how a powerful trinity of forces in Utah — the leading industrial and financial companies, the all-powerful Mormon Church, and the State and local government — were determined that organized labor, especially the IWW, should not get a foothold in the state, and explains the role this played in the final outcome.

Despite the tremendous protest movement in his behalf, Joe Hill was executed, a martyr to the cause of labor. He went to his death protesting his innocence, and his last words were the famous, "Don't mourn. Organize!"

The Case of Joe Hill

BY PHILIP S. FONER

History of the Labor Movement in the United States VOLUME I: *From Colonial Times to the Founding of the American Federation of Labor* VOLUME II: *From the Founding of the American Federation of Labor to the Emergence of American Imperialism* VOLUME III: *The Policies and Practices of the American Federation of Labor, 1900–1909* VOLUME IV: *The Industrial Workers of the World, 1905–1917*

A History of Cuba and Its Relations with the United States (2 vols.)
The Life and Writings of Frederick Douglass (4 vols.)
The Complete Writings of Thomas Paine (2 vols.)
Business and Slavery: The New York Merchants and the Irrepressible Conflict
The Fur and Leather Workers Union
Jack London: American Rebel
Mark Twain: Social Critic
The Jews in American History: 1654–1865
The Basic Writings of Thomas Jefferson
The Selected Writing of George Washington
The Selected Writings of Abraham Lincoln
The Selected Writings of Franklin D. Roosevelt
The Letters of Joe Hill

The Case
of
Joe Hill

by Philip S. Foner

INTERNATIONAL PUBLISHERS
New York

Preface

The case of Joe Hill has been the subject of a celebrated song by Alfred Hayes and Earl Robinson ("Joe Hill"), a novel by Wallace Stegner (*The Preacher and the Slave*), a play by Barrie Stavis (*The Man Who Never Died*).[1] But it has received little or no treatment in standard histories of the American labor movement. Neither Paul F. Brissenden in his *The I.W.W.* nor Selig Perlman and Philip Taft in their *History of Labor in the United States, 1896–1932* mention it. Yet few issues stirred the labor movement, in the United States and abroad, as did this case.

It is the general view of most novelists, playwrights, poets— and, of course, all I.W.W. writers—who have written on the subject, that Joe Hill was an innocent man "framed" on a murder charge. In this view, he was "railroaded" to prison and executed in spite of overwhelming evidence that he was not guilty of the crime attributed to him—that of having, on Saturday night, January 10, 1914, shot and killed John G. Morrison, a Salt Lake City grocery man, and his 17-year-old son, Arling. However, Wallace Stegner and Vernon H. Jensen, both of whom have studied the case, reach an entirely opposite conclusion. They assert that Joe Hill was guilty, or probably guilty, of the crime for which he was tried and executed; the contention that he was the victim of a frame-up, they hold, is simply part of the legend of labor history.[2]

Labor martyr or murderer? Frame-up or legend? The answer lies in an examination of the case of Joe Hill.

My study of the case of Joe Hill began in connection with my work on *The Industrial Workers of the World, 1905–1917* (Volume IV of *History of the Labor Movement in the United States*). However, because of space limitations, I found it impossible to discuss the case in detail in that volume. This, and the fact that the 50th anniversary of Joe Hill's execution (November 19, 1915) was approaching, convinced me that a separate book on this important labor case would be useful.

In the preparation of this study, I have had the assistance of nu-

merous libraries, historical societies and individuals. I wish, espe-
cially, to express my gratitude to the British Museum, the Labadie
Collection, University of Michigan Library, the Royal Ministry of
Foreign Affairs (Stockholm, Sweden), the library of Brigham
Young University, the University of California Library (Berkeley),
the Library of Congress, the National Archives, New York Public
Library, University of Washington Library, the Utah Historical
Society and the Tamiment Institute Library of New York University
and to Louise Heinze, its director. I owe a great debt to the late
Elizabeth Gurley Flynn for permitting me to use letters of Joe Hill
to her and for information obtained during interviews. I wish to
thank Barrie Stavis for permitting me to examine his collection of
Joe Hill material, and Wallace Stegner for permission to use material in the Wallace Stegner Collection, Hoover Institution on War,
Revolution, and Peace Library, Stanford University. I also wish to
thank Harold Cammer and Nathan Witt for reading a draft of the
manuscript and making a number of valuable legal suggestions.

For the convenience of the reader, I have, in a number of cases,
placed explanatory notes at the bottom of the page. In the main,
however, further development of points made in the text will be
found in the reference notes. I have retained throughout the spelling
and punctuation in all original letters and documents.

PHILIP S. FONER

Croton-on-Hudson, New York
July 1965

Contents

I.W.W. Songwriter

In July 1937, when the I.W.W. was only a shell of an organiza-tion, the *One Big Union Monthly,* its official organ, wrote: "One of the things the working class movement is indebted to the I.W.W. for is the teaching of the value of songs in the struggle for emancipa-tion." The I.W.W.'s most accomplished, most famous and most pro-lific songwriter was Joseph Hillstrom, known to millions in every part of the world as Joe Hill.

He was born in Sweden, October 7, 1879, and christened Joel Hägglund. His father was a railroad worker and an amateur or-ganist, but although his son had an opportunity to hear music played in the home, he had no musical training. In 1915, when he was in prison in Salt Lake City, Joe Hill wrote to Katie Phar, a 10-year-old girl who used to sing his songs: "I am glad to hear that you are taking lessons and intend to be a musician. . . . I wish I had a chance to take music lessons when I was a kid, but I was not fortunate enough for that because I had to go to work at the age of 10, when my father died, and I had no money to spare for music lessons, but by trying hard I picked up what little I know about music without lessons. You see I've got music in my blood and it just comes natural to me to play any kind of an instrument."[1]

Joel Hägglund came to the United States from Sweden in 1902 at the age of 23. For ten years he worked at many jobs, during which time he changed his name to Joseph Hillstrom, and became popu-larly known as Joe Hill. He stacked wheat and laid pipe; he played the piano and cleaned spittoons in a Bowery saloon; he dug copper and shipped out; he worked on docks and smelters. And he "scrib-bled." He wrote poems, songs, bits of verse, all kinds of things.

THE I.W.W.

In 1910 Joe Hill joined the I.W.W. local in San Pedro, California. The Industrial Workers of the World was five years old. It had been organized in June 1905 at a convention in Chicago attended by socialists, anarchists, trade unionists, and revolutionaries, among them white-haired Mother Jones, the 75-year-old organizer for the United Mine Workers of America; Eugene V. Debs, leader of the Socialist Party; Daniel De Leon, head of the Socialist Labor Party; Lucy Parsons, widow of the Haymarket Affair martyr, Albert R. Parsons; and William D. ("Big Bill") Haywood, the 36-year-old former cowboy and miner and secretary-treasurer of the militant Western Federation of Miners. Haywood opened the historic convention with the declaration:

"Fellow Workers: This is the Continental Congress of the Working Class. We are here to confederate the workers of this country into a working-class movement in possession of the economic powers, the means of life, in control of the machinery of production and distribution without regard to capitalist masters."

Though the delegates differed on many things, they agreed that the American Federation of Labor, with its craft unionism, class collaboration and "pure and simple" trade unionism, had to be replaced by an organization which stood for industrial unionism, organization of all workers regardless of skill, sex, color or nationality, and the establishment of a new social system to replace capitalism. Where the A.F. of L. called for collaboration between workers and employers, the I.W.W. wrote in the preamble to its constitution:

"The working class and the employing class have nothing in common. There can be no peace so long as hunger and want are found among millions of working people and the few, who make up the employing class, have all the good things of life. Between these two classes, a struggle must go on until the workers of the world organize as a class, take possession of the earth and the machinery of production, and abolish the wage system."

Against the craft unionism of the A.F. of L. (which they called "The American Separation of Labor") the I.W.W. set as its goal, "One Big Union." In keeping with this concept, they organized the skilled and unskilled, foreign-born and native Americans, Negroes and whites, women and men. The Wobblies, as members of the I.W.W. came to be known, were fiercely militant, opposed to contracts with employers, active in strike struggles. The abolition of capitalism would come, they believed, through a series of general strikes, after which the workers would run the industries themselves. "By organizing industrially, we are forming the structure of the new society within the shell of the old."

The I.W.W. went through two splits by 1908 and emerged in that year as a revolutionary industrial union devoted to economic activity, opposed in general to political action, and seeking to achieve its goal of the One Big Union through direct action, sabotage (more often preached than practiced), passive resistance, and labor solidarity. Through spectacular free speech fights and mass strikes, the I.W.W. soon made a name for itself, appreciated by many workers heretofore unorganized and hated by those who wished to maintain low wages, long hours of work, and inhuman working conditions. In general, the I.W.W. after 1908 operated chiefly among the workers whom the A.F. of L. would not and did not reach—the migratory workers of the West in the lumber and construction camps and in the agricultural fields, and the unskilled workers of the East, particularly in the steel and textile mills and rubber and automobile plants—the most poorly paid and the worse treated.[2]

THE LITTLE RED SONG BOOK

Three words epitomized the slogan of the I.W.W.: Emancipation, Education, and Organization. The I.W.W. organized Propaganda Leagues and Industrial Education Clubs. It published hundreds of thousands of leaflets, many illustrated with simple but effective cartoons. It distributed pamphlets and "stickers." But to many Wobblies, especially after 1912, the best educational material published by the I.W.W. was *The Little Red Song Book*. "There are 38 songs in the I.W.W. song book," a Wobbly organizer wrote in 1912, "and out of that number 24 are educational, and I can truthfully say that every one of them is almost a lecture in itself." Some Wobblies even went so far as to recommend that the I.W.W. cease publishing pamphlets and other literature of an economic nature and concentrate solely on the *Song Book*. Although Joe Hill did not endorse such a position, he did argue that "if a person can put a few cold, common-sense facts into a song and dress them (the facts) up in a cloak of humor to take the dryness out of them, he will succeed in reaching a great number of workers who are too unintelligent or too indifferent to read a pamphlet or an editorial on economic science."[3]

In 1911, while working as a dock-walloper in San Pedro, Joe Hill wrote his first known song, "Casey Jones—the Union Scab," a parody of the original Casey Jones song which had appeared two years before. Written to assist the workers on strike on the South Pacific Line who were faced with defeat by the importation of scabs, the famous narrative ballad dealt with a scab who "got a wooden medal for being good and faithful on the S.P. line." It told of the I.W.W.'s sabotage of Casey Jones' engine, his trip to heaven, where

he even "went scabbing on the angels," his descent into hell, and
the ignominious tasks assigned him there:

> *"Casey Jones," the Devil said, "Oh, fine;*
> *Casey Jones, get busy shoveling sulphur;*
> *That's what you get for scabbing on the S.P. line."*

The song was an immediate success. Printed on colored cards
which were sold to help the strike fund, the song helped to keep
the strike alive. Within a few months it was being sung by workers
in many parts of the country, as migratory laborers carried it across
the land. "Casey Jones" is the classic American song about the scab,
and it is as widely known today as in the period when it was written.

Joe Hill soon became one of the leading contributors to the *Little
Red Song Book;* by 1913, he was already the most popular of
the little band of poets and songwriters—which included Richard
Brazier, Ralph Chaplin, Laura Payne Emerson, Covington Hall,
James Connell (author of "The Red Flag"*), and Charles Ash-
leigh—whose works appeared in the pages of the song book. The
"Preacher and the Slave," "Where the Fraser River Flows," "John
Golden and the Lawrence Strike," "Mr. Block," "Scissorbill," "What
We Want," "The Tramp," "There is Power," "The Rebel Girl" (inspired by his affection for Elizabeth Gurley Flynn and which Joe
Hill hoped "will help to line up the women workers in the OBU"),
"Should I Ever Be A Soldier"—were some of the songs of Joe Hill
which became famous as soon as they were published.[4] As their
titles reveal, these songs emerged out of actual conditions and struggles of the workers and were consciously written to be used as
weapons in their struggles.[5] "There is Power in a Union," sung to
the tune of the hymn, "There is Power in the Blood," put the
I.W.W.'s philosophy in a nutshell:

> *There is pow'r, there is pow'r*
> *In a band of workingmen,*
> *When they stand hand in hand*
> *There's a pow'r that's a pow'r*
> *That must rule in every land—*
> *One Industrial Union Grand.*

---

* Connell, an Irish Socialist, composed "The Red Flag" during the London
dock strike of 1889. Connell's original tune was "The White Cockade," but
when taken over intact by the I.W.W. from the British labor movement,
"The Red Flag" soon became attached to "Maryland, My Maryland."

Joe Hill's classic, "The Preacher and the Slave" ("Pie in the Sky"), composed about 1911, summed up the rivalry between the Wobblies and the Salvation Army for the allegiance of the migratory workers, and effectively exposed the hypocrisy of the church. This parody of "The Sweet Bye and Bye" is a devastating attack on "long-haired preachers who come out every night":

> *Try to tell you what's wrong and what's right;*
> *But when asked how 'bout something to eat;*
> *They will answer with voices so sweet:*
>
>   Chorus
> *You will eat, bye and bye,*
> *In that glorious land above the sky; (Way up high)*
> *Work and pray, live on hay.*
> *You'll get pie in the sky when you die.* (That's no lie.)*

Joe Hill's songs were sung on numerous picket lines during the heyday of the I.W.W. When the striking hop workers at Wheatland were attacked by the sheriff's posse, they were singing Joe Hill's "Mr. Block," specifically the verse in which Block, a migratory worker whose head was "made of lumber and solid as a rock," found a job one day. After paying seven dollars to the "Shark" (the employment agents) for fare and fee, he was shipped to a desert, where he discovered he had been fooled:

> *Block hiked back to the city, but wasn't*
> *doing well.*
> *He said, "I'll join the union—the great A.F.*
> *of L."*
> *He got a job next morning, got fired in the*
> *night.*
> *He said, "I'll see Sam Gompers and he'll fix that*
> *foreman right."*
> *Sam Gompers said, "You see,*
> *You've got our sympathy."*

In the Wheatland trial, the prosecuting attorney charged that "the song itself was a disgrace to organized labor and a slam at the name of Samuel Gompers." This remark helped to make "Mr. Block"

---

* Joe Ettor, I.W.W. organizer, spelled out the same idea when he said: "We have no objection to the saving of souls after death. Our object is to save souls and bodies while the people are alive." (*Solidarity,* Dec. 28, 1912.)

A page from the original sheet music by Joe Hill for "The Rebel Girl," which he presented to Elizabeth Gurley Flynn and dedicated to her. The dedication in Joe Hill's handwriting is from the cover.

14

famous, as did the fact that it was sung at all defense meetings for Ford and Suhr, I.W.W. defendants in the Wheatland murder trial. "Of all the songs [of the I.W.W.]," noted a California journalist early in 1914, "the greatest favorite now is 'Mr. Block.'"[6]

In her tribute to Joe Hill as a songwriter, published in the May 22, 1915, issue of *Solidarity,* Elizabeth Gurley Flynn wrote:

"Joe writes songs that sing, that lilt and laugh and sparkle, that kindle the fires of revolt in the most crushed spirit and quicken the desire for fuller life in the most humble slave. He has put into words the inarticulate craving of 'the sailor, and the tailor and the lumberjack' for freedom, nor does he forget 'the pretty girls that's making curls.'* He has expressed the manifold phrases of our propaganda from the gay of Mr. Block and Casey Jones to the grave of 'Should a gun I ever shoulder, 'tis to crush the tyrant's might.' He has crystallized the organization's spirit into imperishable forms, songs of the people—folk songs."

* This is a quotation from Joe Hill's song, "What We Want":
> "We want the sailor and the tailor and the lumberjacks,
> And all the cooks and laundry girls;
> We want the guy that dives for pearls,
> The pretty maid that's making curls,
> And the baker and the staker and the chimneysweep;
> We want the man that's slinging hash
> The child that works for little cash
> In One Union grand."

CHAPTER TWO

The Murders and the Arrest

In the years after 1910, Joe Hill was an I.W.W. "boomer," a traveler from railroad yard to fruit camp to dock front. Carrying an I.W.W. card from the San Pedro, California, local, he moved from one Wobbly meeting hall to the next, helping out in strikes and free speech fights, fighting with the Mexican revolutionaries in the Battle of Mexicali in which he is said to have been shot in the leg,[1] working at various trades, most often as a mechanic, and, of course, always composing his songs. He was severely beaten by vigilantes during the great free speech fight in San Diego, California, in 1912. He was one of the speakers at the huge protest meeting sponsored by the Los Angeles A.F. of L. Central Labor Council. "He explained," one reporter wrote, "that he had just come from the hospitality of the M & M in San Diego, that owing to that hospitality he was physically unable to make any lengthy speech. He looked as though he had just risen from a sick bed."[2] The "M & M" was the open-shop Manufacturers' and Merchants' Association.

LABOR STRUGGLES IN UTAH

In the fall of 1913, Joe Hill was in Utah. The Mormon Commonwealth had been the scene of bitter labor struggles ever since the summer of 1912. In September, 1912, the Western Federation of Miners began a strike to organize the mines of Bingham Canyon, acknowledged to be "the most repulsive mining camp" in the United States. The Utah Copper Co., the main employer at Bingham, hired an "army" of gunmen to protect the strikebreakers it imported into the Canyon. Governor William Spry of Utah, who was to play a crucial role in the Joe Hill case, allowed the company a free hand in importing scabs and permitted it to deputize its gunmen as sheriffs. (Governor Spry had already performed a service for the copper companies by vetoing a bill, passed by both houses of the Utah legislature, making a coroner's investigation of death in the mines obligatory. The miners referred to Spry as "the jumping-jack of the copper kings.") The strike was called off in October, and Bingham Canyon continued as an open shop.[3]

Meanwhile, I.W.W. Local 69, Salt Lake City, with Ed Rowan as secretary, was conducting an intensive organizing campaign among the construction workers employed by the Utah Construction Co. In June 1913, 1,500 workers on the Denver Rio Grande Railroad construction project between Soldiers Summit and Tucker, Utah, went out on strike for a wage increase of 25 per cent and a reduction of hours from ten to nine. The Utah Construction Co., the main contractor, tried to emulate the Utah Copper Co. by hiring gunmen and importing strikebreakers. The strike leaders were arrested and imprisoned and many strikers were forcibly deported. But this time the strike-breaking strategy failed because of the support given the strikers by the trainmen of the D.R.G. They refused to allow anyone to ride over the line unless they had I.W.W. cards or could produce a pass from the strike committee. After three weeks, the Utah Construction Co. was forced to give in to the strikers' demands.[4]

Years later a member of the strike committee recalled that after the strikers' victory a Utah Construction official had said: "You I.W.W.'s caught us with our pants down this time, but I can assure you that before the end of a year every damn single I.W.W. will be run out of the state of Utah."[5] The victory at Tucker was followed by a well-organized assault upon the I.W.W. Wobbly street meetings in Salt Lake City and other Utah communities were broken up, the speakers assaulted and jailed. On August 12, 1913, a group of thugs, some of whom were special deputies of the Utah Construction Co. and the Utah Copper Co., deliberately and violently routed an I.W.W. street meeting, attacking the Wobbly leaders with gun butts. The attack was obviously planned by local police authorities. Patrolmen, detectives and the police chief arrived on the scene before the riot began, and three physicians were in waiting in the police emergency hospital to care for the expected victims. It is symbolic of the attitude of officials in Salt Lake City that James F. Morgan, the principal Wobbly speaker, was charged with attempting to murder Axel Steel, leader of the armed mob. Despite its attacks on the I.W.W., the Salt Lake press acknowledged that Steele, not Morgan, was the aggressor; nevertheless, the Wobbly leader, not the armed mobster, was jailed. Other Wobblies were given short sentence for inciting to riot.

The chief of police declared war on Local 69, and I.W.W. meetings were broken up throughout the summer. The Wobblies called for free-speech fighters from the neighboring states. They began to come in, mainly from Colorado and California, and Joe Hill was among them.[6]

A Wobbly who had been on the picket line in the D.R.G. strike declared many years later that Joe Hill had picketed with him.[7] Hill himself never said as much. His only reference to his activity in Utah before coming to the neighborhood of Salt Lake City was the statement: "Shortly before my arrest I came down from Park City, where I was working in the mines."[8] I.W.W. writers have described Hill as "working and organizing in Bingham Canyon."[9] Vernon H. Jensen, on the other hand, dismisses Joe Hill's claim to have been in the mines in Park City, since there "is no proof of it."[10] But, following a careful investigation, the Deseret *Evening News* reported on January 15 that "Applequist and Hillstrom had . . . worked at Park City as machinists in the Silver King mines." That much, then, appears certain.

Through Otto Applequist, Joe Hill was introduced to Swedish families in Sandy. He renewed acquaintance with members of the Eselius family in Murray, a town about 12 miles from Salt Lake City. It was at the Eselius' boarding house that Joe Hill was arrested. Three of the Eselius brothers had worked with Hill in California, and he paid them regular visits. However, he was not living at the Eselius house. Mrs. Betty Eeselius Olsen testified at his trial that "He was just a visitor there, just came there on account of his music, he was musical."

THE MURDERS

On Saturday, January 10, 1914, at about 9:45 P.M., two armed men, masked with red bandana handkerchiefs, entered John G. Morrison's grocery store at 778 South West Temple Street in Salt Lake City. The grocery man and his two sons, Arling, age 17, and Merlin, age 14, were alone in the store and closing for the night. Only one version of what followed was ever obtainable—that of Merlin Morrison, and his story was reported differently in three Salt Lake City newspapers during the next few days. As one pieces these accounts together, it appears that the two men rushed toward John G. Morrison as soon as they entered, and shouted, "We've got you now." One of the men then opened fire on the elder Morrison. Merlin, frightened, hid behind some shelves in the back of the store, "but I kept my head out far enough to see it all." Although he changed this account several times, he reported that, as his father fell, his brother

Arling seized a revolver and opened fire on the masked men. "I think the bullet hit one man. They wheeled and fired at my brother three times." Arling was instantly killed, and the father died that night, leaving no clue about his murderers. He had been shot twice.

The assailants fled, taking nothing, and the boy ran from behind one of the rear counters, and phoned the police, to tell them, "in a hysterical, high-pitched voice, that his father and brother had been killed."[11]

"Motive Probably Revenge," the Deseret *Evening News* announced on January 12, 1914. "The generally accepted theory," it continued, "is that the highwaymen who were routed by J. G. Morrison on two occasions within the past 10 years when they were fired upon by Morrison and forced into street battles with the fearless grocer and the police, returned to the Morrison store and killed the proprietor through revenge." The daily newspaper operated by the Mormon Church was referring to previous encounters Morrison had had with bandits. He had foiled an attempted robbery in 1903 by shooting at his assailants, wounding one of them seriously. Again, on September 20, 1913, he had been held up by two masked men and had forced them to flee amid a hail of bullets. It was thus generally believed that the same men who had participated in the two previously thwarted attempts to rob Morrison had returned on January 10, 1914, to take his life in revenge. Furthermore, Morrison had been a member of the Salt Lake City police force some years earlier. A few days before his death, he had told Police Captain Hempel that he was in constant dread of men he had arrested, and that he regretted that he "ever was a member of the force." Mrs. Morrison told the police that her husband had spoken to her of two men in the neighborhood whom he regarded as enemies, had divulged their names to her, and had said, "If anything ever happens to me, you may have to look them up."[12]

A description of the bandits—as reported in the press, and based on Merlin's statements—gave the height of both as 5 feet 9 inches and weighing about 155 pounds. (But Merlin's account changed so often that on January 13, 1914, the Deseret *Evening News* noted that "The descriptions were mixed by the repeated telling of the story by Merlin Morrison.") Two neighbors, who said they had seen two men walking up the street a short time before the shooting, were reported to have told the sheriff that one of the men was about 5 feet 9 inches and weighed about 160 pounds.[13]

A trail of blood was traced several blocks from an alley near the store to a vacant lot and then to the D.R.G. railroad tracks, where it was lost. A large blood clot, believed to have been coughed up from a lung wound, was also found. It was assumed that the blood came from one of the bandits, who was judged to have been wounded by Arling. The character of the trail led the Deseret *Evening News* to conclude that the wounded man was "evidently weak and staggering from loss of blood."[14]

Various suspects were arrested. One picked up near the murder scene was a 26-year-old restaurant helper named W. J. Williams who was found with a blood-stained handkerchief. "The description of Williams tallies in a general way with that of one of the murderers," the Salt Lake *Tribune* announced. The police sought Frank Z. Wilson, who had just finished a penitentiary term which followed an arrest in which Morrison, then a police officer, had taken part. No effort, however, was made to hold the two men whom Morrison had told his wife were his enemies. "They are said to be taxpayers of the district and in business in the neighborhood," the Deseret *Evening News* noted in explaining the police's reluctance to consider them as suspects.[15]

All the suspects picked up in the days immediately following the murders were later released, save one—Joe Hill.

ARREST OF JOE HILL

Between 11 and 11:30 P.M. of the night Morrison and his son were murdered, Joe Hill appeared at the office of Dr. Frank McHugh, about five or six miles from the Morrison grocery store.* He was seeking treatment for a gunshot wound in his left side. A bullet had entered his chest an inch below the heart, cut through the bottom part of his left lung, and passed out through his back. "I asked him how he came to be shot," Dr. McHugh related three days later, "and he told me that he and another fellow had quarrelled over a girl and that he had struck the other man, who retaliated by shooting him." Hill told Dr. McHugh that he was as much to blame as the other fellow, and wanted the affair kept quiet.[16]

---

* Vernon H. Jensen asserts that the office was "about two and one-half miles from the scene of the murder." ("The Legend of Joe Hill," *Industrial and Labor Relations Review*, Vol. IV, April 1951, p. 378.) James O. Morris also makes this estimate. ("The Case of Joe Hill," unpublished manuscript, June 1950, Labadie Collection, University of Michigan Library, p. 10.) But the Deseret *Evening News* placed it at "six miles or so distant." (Jan. 14, 1914.)

Dr. McHugh dressed the wound, and Joe Hill was driven to the Eselius' boarding house in Murray by Dr. A. A. Bird, who had happened to pass by. Hill had a gun with him when he visited Dr. McHugh to have his wound dressed; but on the trip to Murray, when Dr. Bird got out to crank his car after some engine trouble, he threw the gun away. Hill never clearly explained why he had disposed of his gun, but he insisted that the weapon was a .32-caliber Luger automatic—and Morrison was killed by a .38-caliber automatic pistol, probably a Colt.[17]

Three days after Hill's visit to his office, Dr. McHugh went to the Salt Lake authorities and told them that Joseph Hillstrom, with whom he was personally acquainted, had come to his home late Saturday night for medical attention. The authorities notified Murray chief of police Fred Peters, who set out to arrest Hill. To make it easier for the police to do so, Dr. McHugh said he would give Hill a "shot" of morphine so that he would be asleep or in a drugged condition.* The chief of police and three policemen broke into Joe Hill's room, and, as Peters recounted it, the suspect leaped out of bed when they entered, and reached under the pillow as though to get a gun. As he did, Peters stated, he shot him through the hand and placed him under arrest. Joe Hill's version of how he was shot and treated after he was arrested was quite different:

"As I was laying there half asleep, when I was aroused by a knock on the door, somebody opened the door and in came four men with revolvers in their hands. A shot rang out and a bullet passed right over my chest, grazing my shoulder and penetrating my right hand through my knuckles, crippling me for life. There was no need of shooting and at that time because I was helpless as a baby and had no weapons of any kind. The only thing that saved my life at that time was the officer's inefficiency with firearms.

"I was then brought up to the county jail where I was given a bunk and went to sleep immediately. The next morning I was pretty sore on account of being shot in three places. I asked to be taken to a hospital but was instead taken upstairs to a solitary cell, and told that I was charged with murder and had better confess right away. I did not know anything about any murder and told them so. They still insisted on that I confess and told me they would

---

* During Hill's trial, Dr. McHugh testified that he had given Hill the shot of morphine "so that he would be arrested without hurting himself or hurting anyone else." (Deseret *Evening News*, June 22, 1914; Salt Lake *Tribune*, June 23, 1914.)

take me to a hospital and 'treat me white' if I did. I told them I knew nothing of any murder. They called me a 'liar' and after that I refused to answer any questions. I grew weaker and weaker and for three or four days I was hovering between life and death and I remember an officer coming up and telling me that according to the doctor's statement I only had one more hour to live. . . . I finally 'pulled through' because I made up my mind not to die."[18]

There is little doubt that Hill's version is a correct one. For one thing, there was no gun under his pillow or anywhere else in the room. In addition, he had been drugged (remaining in a stupor for several hours after his arrest) and severely wounded. It is hardly possible that he could have "leaped" or made any effort to prevent the police from arresting him.

While the police never acknowledged using the "third-degree methods" Hill describes to get him to confess, there is evidence that they did use illegal means in an attempt to secure a confession. Mrs. Betty Eselius Olsen testified that on the day Hill was arrested, certain officers entered her home; they told her Hill had confessed to giving her his gun, and asked her to produce it. She was aware of the deception, for she had no knowledge of the weapon and was sure Hill had said nothing about one, and she told the police several times that she knew nothing about a gun. Thereupon, the police took Robert Erickson, Mrs. Olsen's son, to headquarters for "questioning." The police promised Mrs. Olsen that if she agreed to confer with Hill and secure a confession, they would release her son. She went to Hill with this purpose in mind, but he told her he had nothing to confess. Although the police released her son, their conduct reveals the lengths to which the law enforcement authorities were ready to go in order to pin the murder on Joe Hill.[19]

No confession was ever obtained. Joe Hill told the police that he had thrown his gun away en route to Murray in Dr. Bird's car; that he was shot in a dispute over a woman whom he did not wish to identify lest her reputation be ruined; and that he was innocent of the murder of Morrison and his son.

A note signed "Otto" was found on Hill's person when he was arrested. This simply read: "Hilda and I and Christina were here. We went to the Empress. Tried to find you." The police started a search for Applequist on the supposition that he was one of the murderers. A photo of Applequist's face was shown to all of the witnesses at or near the scene of the murder, but none recognized him. According to the Eselius brothers, Applequist left Murray because he was "down and out and dead broke." At any rate, the quest for him was futile. He was never seen again.[20]

PRELIMINARY HEARING

Joe Hill pleaded "Not Guilty" on January 22 to the charge of having murdered J. G. Morrison, and a preliminary hearing was held six days later before Justice of the Peace Harry S. Harper to determine whether there was sufficient evidence to warrant keeping Hill in custody.[21] Having no money to hire counsel, Hill acted as his own attorney both when arraigned and at the preliminary hearing. ("When searched at the county jail, $5.60 in money and a note were taken from him [Hill]," the Deseret *Evening News* reported on January 14, 1914. The note was the one from Otto Applequist.) Hill presented no witnesses of his own, but cross-examined the state's witnesses briefly. None of them identified Hill as one of the killers, but some of the witnesses spoke of the similarities between one of the two men and the defendant. The Salt Lake City papers did not report fully on the hearing, and the official record has disappeared. However, Joe Hill later quoted from the record in his letter to the Utah Pardon Board,* and no one questioned the accuracy of his quotations. Hill asked Merlin, who stated that Joe Hill's height and size were about the same as the man he saw in the store, "When you saw me in the jail this morning after my arrest, did you not say, 'No, that is not the man at all. The ones I saw were shorter and heavier.'" Merlin denied having ever said this, and Hill dropped the cross-examination, although he always insisted that Merlin had been persuaded by the police to repudiate his first comment when he saw him.[22]

Mrs. Phoebe Seeley, who (with her husband) had seen two men near the store just before the murders, would not say Hill resembled, in the slightest sense, the taller of them. She first described the man as having "small features and light bushy hair." Thereupon, the magistrate suggested, "You mean medium colored hair like Mr. Hillstrom's don't you?" The witness, under this prodding, apparently answered in the affirmative. But when the magistrate continued with the question, "Is the general appearance of Mr. Hillstrom anything like the man you saw?" the witness replied, "No, I won't,—no, I can't say that." Hill objected to the leading questions put to Mrs. Seeley, but was overruled.

* *See below,* pp. 79–81.

Mrs. Nettie Mahan and Mrs. Vera Hanson, neighbors of the
Morrisons, both testified for the state, and indicated that they had
seen a man escaping the murder scene; that he ran in a stooped
position with his hands clutching his chest. Mrs. Hanson said he
had cried out, "Bob" or "Oh, Bob!" Hill asked her if she could
identify him as that man, and if she could say his voice and the
voice of the fleeing man were the same. "No, I could not," said
Mrs. Hanson. Mrs. Mahan thought she heard the man say, "I'm
shot," but she was not at all certain he had.[23]

Drs. McHugh and Bird told their stories. Testimony about
bullets was given, none of which specifically pinned the murder on
Hill. Two red bandana handkerchiefs were placed in evidence
against Hill. One of them had been found in a barn about two
blocks from the store; the other came from Hill's room in Murray.
The ludicrousness of charging that Hill wore both of them concerned neither the county attorney nor the press. In a brief closing
argument, Hill retorted: "I have only this to say. I fail utterly to see
how any significance can attach to the discovery of a red bandana
handkerchief such as I owned. Many persons have red handkerchiefs and it is no uncommon thing to lose them."[24]

The evidence adduced against Hill in the preliminary hearing was
deemed sufficient for prosecution, and he was bound over to the
Third District Court for trial, denied bail, and, pending the opening of the trial, returned to the county jail. Later, he was arraigned
before Judge Morris L. Ritchie, who read the indictment to him.
He pleaded not guilty to the charge of first degree murder of
Morrison. (He was not charged with the murder of Arling.) The
trial was scheduled to begin on June 10.

In the meantime, Hill had secured attorneys. A few days after the
preliminary hearing, E. E. McDougall, an out-of-state attorney, came
to see Hill, and volunteered to defend him without charge. "Seeing
that the proposition was in perfect harmony with my bankroll,"
Hill later recounted, "I accepted his offer."[25] McDougall obtained
the services of Frank B. Scott as associate counsel.

Joe Hill felt confident of being exonerated, having closed his argument at the preliminary hearing with the statement that he would
present his witnesses in the District Court. This confidence continued. In May, he wrote Katie Phar, the young singer of his songs
and daughter of a Spokane I.W.W. member: "My case is coming
up this month, and everything looks good."[26]

There appears to be a sound basis for Hill's feeling of confidence.

Only his gun wound circumstantially linked him with the murders. It had not been established at the preliminary hearing that Morrison's gun had been fired. Though the doctors testified that the bullet which wounded Hill passed completely through his body, no bullet was found in the store that could have done this. There were six steel-jacketed bullets found, two near Morrison's body and four near Arling's; but the Morrison gun shot only plain lead bullets. Since the bullet which struck Hill had gone all the way through his body, a lead bullet should have been found in the store, if that was where his wound had been inflicted. But though the police inspected the store several times, no lead bullet was ever found.

No blood other than the dead man's was found in the store. There was no motive established to explain why Hill should have been the murderer. There had been no robbery attempt. The police attached great significance to the red bandana handkerchief found in Hill's room. But literally millions of American workers owned similar bandanas. In short, apart from the fact that Hill had been shot and wounded on the same night as the murders, all the details brought out at the preliminary hearing pointed to the fact that he was not guilty.

HILL FOUND GUILTY BEFORE TRIAL

But a campaign to find him guilty had been under way outside the courtroom from the moment Joe Hill was arrested. On the very day of the arrest, the police released their verdict: "The police now believe that the circumstantial evidence all points to the guilt of Hill. . . . The police regard the story told by Hill as improbable."[27]

The Deseret *Evening News* of January 24, 1914, under the headline "Hillstrom's Crime Record in California Sent Here," told the story, furnished by the police, that Hill had been arrested in Los Angeles in June, 1913, and "accused of participation in street car holdups." Even though no conviction was noted, the picture presented to the public from then on was that Joe Hill was a seasoned criminal. The press descriptions of Hill in court during the arraignment were designed to portray him as a long-time criminal. "In the courtroom," went one description, "Hillstrom wore a hardened look, betraying no nervousness, his features showing no emotion; and he seemed callous to what was going on."[28] Hill's role as his own attorney was even used. A reporter wrote: "His conduct as an attorney convinced the state's attorneys that he was more or less familiar with court procedure, and they regarded the brevity of his appeal as shrewdness rather than owing to a lack of knowledge."[29]

Hill maintained a tight-lipped silence while his past was being distorted, creating an atmosphere in Salt Lake City that was hardly conducive to a fair trial. But later he did issue a statement denying any connection with previous arrests except one:

"In spite of all the hideous pictures and all the bad things said and printed about me,* I had only been arrested once before in my life, and that was in San Pedro, Calif. at the time of the stevedores' and dock workers' strike. I was secretary of the strike committee, and I suppose I was a little too active to suit the chief of the burg, so he arrested me and gave me 30 days in the city jail for 'vagrancy'—and there you have the full extent of my 'criminal record.'

"I have always worked hard for a living and paid for everything I got, and my spare time I spend by painting pictures, writing songs and composing music."[30]

If the police and the press did not know that Joe Hill was a militant I.W.W. member when he was arrested, they learned of it after the report of the San Pedro officers. A dispatch from San Francisco, dated April 7, noted: "They the police wrote to San Pedro, Calif., where Hill worked among the transport workers, in an endeavor to get something against him. The chief of police informed them that Hill was an undesirable citizen, an alien in this country without warrant of law, and that he was a dangerous character. To prove which the chief stated that Hill was an I.W.W. agitator and the author of I.W.W. songs. What more is needed to convict him?" Scott and McDougall, Hill's attorneys, made the same point, writing in the I.W.W. journals in May: "The main thing the state has against Hill is that he is an I.W.W. and therefore *must be guilty*. Hill tried to keep the I.W.W. out of it and denied it, but the papers fastened it on him."[31]

The press coupled Hill's reputation as a writer of "inflammatory" and "sacrilegious" songs with his career as a criminal.[32] In mid-March, 1914, the Deseret *Evening News* carried a series of articles

* Hill probably refers to a picture printed in the Deseret *Evening News* of Jan. 24, 1914; it was said to be a "Bertillon photograph" supplied by the Los Angeles police and to show Hill after he was arrested as "a car robbery suspect." The picture was denounced by Hill's friends as "false," and the paper never reprinted it. But the first publication had already done the damage. In the first reports of Hill's arrest, he was confused with Frank Z. Wilson, who had just served a term in the Utah state prison. (Deseret *Evening News*, Jan. 14, 1914.)

on the dangers facing Salt Lake City from the I.W.W. and its doctrines of "destruction."[33] The I.W.W. claimed that the series was inspired by the Utah Construction Co. and the Utah Copper Co. as part of a conspiracy to railroad Hill to his death.[34] While this charge is not susceptible to proof, it is difficult to imagine that the men who later served on the Joe Hill jury had not read all of these stories and were not influenced by them.

It should also be noted that two days after the murders, the Deseret *Evening News* emphasized that the slaying of Morrison and his son was the "culmination of a Series of Bold Crimes," and noted that Salt Lake citizens were growing apprehensive over the failure of the police to track down the perpetrators of the crimes that were plaguing the city.[35] Joe Hill offered an easy solution to this problem. He was penniless, seemingly friendless, a homeless man, and an I.W.W. agitator to boot. It was not difficult to convince a jury that the convenient fact that he had been wounded on the same night was enough to send such a man to his death. It is significant that after Hill was arrested, the police gave up even the pretense of searching for other suspects, and released the four men already held.

In a sense, the trial was to be anti-climactical. The police department and the press had found Joe Hill guilty long before the trial date approached.

CHAPTER THREE

The Trial

The State of Utah vs. Joseph Hillstrom, the trial for the life of
Joe Hill, began on June 10, 1914. The official transcript of the first
13 days' proceedings, including the interrogation of the jurymen and
the evidence introduced by the state, has disappeared from the
office of the clerk of the Third District Court of Salt Lake City. For
this crucial material, the present-day student must rely on the contemporary newspaper reports, a summary in *State vs. Hillstrom,*
150 Pacific Reporter, pp. 935–49, the text of the Appellant's Brief in
the Supreme Court of the State of Utah, and the opinion of that
court.*

THE JURY

Judge M. L. Ritchie, before whom the case was to be tried, showed
his bias against the defendant early in the proceedings. He repeatedly
"criticized the methods of counsel for the defendant in examining
the prospective jurors," and publicly fumed while the defense attorneys, Scott and McDougall, sought to assure the defendant an
impartial jury. When the defense had exhausted its peremptory
challenges, Judge Ritchie approved a juryman, John G. Ryan, after
it had been revealed that his father had been murdered "by the
same means as that of Mr. Morrison." "His own experience," argued
the defense, "would always rise up and persuade him to resolve every
circumstance against the defendant." Judge Ritchie failed to see any
logic in the argument, and urged the defense to get on with the
trial.[1] Finally, his patience worn thin by the stubborn questioning
of Ryan, Judge Ritchie, while sustaining the defense challenge, burst
out:

"I am thoroughly convinced that . . . *he was a fair and impartial
juror,* and that he did come within the definition laid down by the

* Volume II, "Transcript of the witness introduced on behalf of the de-
fendant," and including the court's instruction to the Jury, is still available in
Salt Lake County. A copy of the Appellant's Brief, comprising 56 pages, is in
File 2573, "Joseph Hillstrom," Woodrow Wilson Papers, Library of Congress.

statute *that he could, notwithstanding the opinion he had formed, act fairly and impartially, obliged to sustain the challenge. . . .* To my mind it was a most absurd performance. If we can examine a juror for an hour . . . there is no limit to prevent us spending a day or a week on one juror until he has finally reached such a state either that his mentality is tired or until he is utterly tired by the subtleties presented."[2]

The Salt Lake *Tribune* noted with satisfaction: "The remarks of the Judge were apparently productive of results, for the twelfth juror was obtained a few minutes later." Of the "twelve men tried and true," one was a laborer and one a motorman. The rest were a real estate dealer, a collector, two farmers, an owner of a blacksmith shop, a clerk, a coal dealer, an owner of a teamster business, a contractor, and a salesman.[3]

THE STATE'S CASE

"The state will rely on circumstantial evidence," the Salt Lake *Tribune* informed the people of Utah on the eve of the trial. "Hillstrom was taken the day after the murder. He was suffering from a gunshot wound in the breast. It was known that Arling Morrison, who was murdered with his father, wounded one of the robbers in the fight."[4] There are three errors in this brief statement. Joe Hill was arrested three days after the murder; it was yet to be conclusively established that Arling had wounded one of the gunmen, and it was anything but clear that the men who had entered Morrison's store had done so to rob him. But the *Tribune* was correct in predicting that the state would rely only on circumstantial evidence. In his opening statement to the jury, District Attorney E. O. Leatherwood declared that he would not directly prove that Hill killed Morrison, but would submit a chain of circumstantial facts from which guilt could be inferred. Specifically, he would prove that a tall and a short man were seen near the store a few minutes before the murder, and that Hill was the taller one; that Arling fired at the men and wounded Hill, who staggered from the store and yelled, "Oh Bob, I'm shot;" that he was treated for a gunshot wound shortly after the murder, and that he carried a .38-caliber Colt automatic, the type used in the murder, into the office of Dr. McHugh.[5]

The case against Joe Hill stood or fell on the identification of the two men who entered Morrison's store. Yet none of the witnesses for the state identified Joe Hill as being one of those two men. The

closest the prosecution came to such "identification" was in the testimony of Merlin Morrison. Indeed, the Salt Lake *Tribune* conceded
that the state's case rested almost exclusively on this testimony: "If
Joseph Hillstrom is convicted of the murder of J. G. Morrison and
his son Arling Morrison,* it will undoubtedly be due in large
measure to the story told on the witness stand in the district court
yesterday by Merlin Morrison, aged 13 years. . . . Being the only eye
witness, the boy's story is the most important bit of testimony the
state has to offer."[6] Here are Merlin's answers to the prosecuting
attorney's obviously leading questions, as reported in the Salt Lake
Herald-Republican:

"Q. How is his [Hill's] height as compared with that of the
taller of the men who entered the store on the night of the shooting?

A. It is about the same as that of the man who fired the shot at
my father.

Q. Does the general appearance of Hillstrom resemble that of the
taller man?

A. He looks the same.

Q. How does the shape of the defendant's head compare with
that of the taller man?

A. It is about the same.

Q. Does the man's general appearance correspond with that of
the man who shot your father?

A. Yes, sir."[7]

The Salt Lake *Tribune* described this testimony as a "positive
identification,"[8] but even the Deseret *Evening News,* hostile though
it was to Joe Hill, conceded that this was far from the case:

*"Merlin Morrison could not identify Hillstrom as being the taller
of the two bandits who held up the store and shot Mr. Morrison. . . .
The boy could not identify the man's features because the taller of
the bandits wore a red handkerchief over the lower part of his face
and his hat was pulled over his eyes, the boy said."*[9]

With Merlin, the only person who saw even a part of the murder,
unable to make a positive identification, the state relied mainly on
the testimony of Mrs. Phoebe Seeley. The very same woman who,
at the preliminary hearing found it impossible to compare Hill and
the tall man she saw even in general appearance, now was convinced
of a striking resemblance between them. She and her husband were
walking near the store before the murder. They passed two men,

* Hill was, of course, on trial only for the slaying of J. G. Morrison.

one tall, the other short. The taller man crowded her off the sidewalk; they exchanged glances, each looking the other directly in the face. Within that short time, and although darkness had fallen long before, she noticed the most minute features. She knew the color of his hair and remembered observing scars on his neck, described his hat and said that he wore a red handkerchief around his neck. Since the Utah Supreme Court relied heavily on her testimony, it is worth examining it in some detail.

"Q. Did this man that turned, the taller of the two, did he look directly at you?

A. Yes.

Q. And did you look directly at him?

A. Yes.

Q. Did you notice anything peculiar about the features of the face of the men. . . . ?

A. Yes.

Q. I wish you would just tell in your own way, Mrs. Seeley, what there was about the face of that man that attracted you.

A. Well, his face was real thin; he had a sharp nose, and rather large nostrils. He had a defection the side of his face or neck.

Q. On the side of the face or neck?

A. Right here on this face.

Q. What do you mean by that—apparently a scar?

A. Yes; it looked as though it might be a scar.

Q. And you observed that?

A. Yes, sir.

Q. Did the nose appear to be particularly sharp that you saw on the tall man there at that time?

A. Yes.

Q. And the nostrils were peculiar?

A. Yes; the gentleman that I met was a sharpfaced man with a real sharp nose, and his nostrils were rather large. . . .

Q. How does the nose of Mr. Hillstrom compare with the nose of the man looked at there?

A. Very much the same.

Q. How do the marks, especially upon the left-hand side of his face and neck, that you have an opportunity to observe, correspond with the marks on the man that you saw there at that time?

A. Well, they look a great deal alike to me. . . ."

Even though Leatherwood helped Mrs. Seeley along with her testimony, he could only get her to say that Hill's nose and that of

the man she had seen was "very much the same," and that the
marks on their necks "look a great deal alike to me." Thereupon,
Judge Ritchie lent the prosecutor a hand and proceeded to question
Mrs. Seeley:

"Q. How does Mr. Hillstrom, as he sits here, compare in regard
to his thinness with the man you saw that day?

A. His thinness is about the same, but his hair—

Q. Just about as thin, had you finished your answer?

A. But his hair is entirely different.*

Q. How does he compare in thinness of the body with the man
you saw that day?

A. I never paid any particular attention.

Q. You did not pay any attention to the thinness of the body, but
the thinness of his face is just the same as the man you saw?

A. Just the same."[10]

Through the deliberate leading of the Judge, the witness's phrase,
"*about the same*" was changed to "*just the same*." In the end, Mrs.
Seeley, like every witness for the prosecution, "would not testify
positively that the man she saw was the defendant." Indeed, she
confessed an honest doubt that he was.[11]

It is obvious that in so short a time no one could have seen so
much as Mrs. Seeley claimed she saw that night. Moreover, in light
of the fact that she had so completely reversed her testimony since
the preliminary hearing, it should be clear that forces were at work
to get her to build a case against Joe Hill.[12]

Mrs. Seeley was not the only witness to alter testimony between
January and June. Mrs. Vera Hansen ran out of her house, directly
across the street from the store, after she heard several shots. She
reached the sidewalk in time to hear the man shout, "Oh, Bob!"
The voice, full of anguish and pain, which had uttered only two
words, she testified, was "the same as the voice of Hillstrom she
heard . . . at the county jail several days after the murder." At the
preliminary hearing, the same witness had said they were not
identical. Serious defense objections that the witness was not quali-
fied as competent to judge voices was overruled by Judge Ritchie.[13]

At the preliminary hearing, Mrs. Hansen stated that she was
unable to identify Hill as the "tall man," but at the trial she was
more cooperative. Although the man she had seen ran in a stooped

* At the preliminary hearing Mrs. Seeley testified that the man she had
seen "had small features and light bushy hair" and did not, in these respects,
resemble Hill.

position, both hands to his chest, she had computed his height positively:

"Q. How did his [Hill's] height and how does his height now, Mrs. Hansen, compare with the man that you saw come out of Morrison's store?

A. Compare exactly."[14]

Mrs. Nellie Mahan viewed the escape from a front-room window of her home. At the preliminary hearing, she was not fully confident that the man had said, "I'm shot." At the trial, she was no longer in doubt. Although she had heard several other men conversing behind her home, she could not distinguish what they said. The man's coat was dark, his hat "soft." Did this man resemble Hillstrom? "Well, all I can say is that the man I saw running was very tall and very thin, and Mr. Hillstrom is very tall and very thin."[15]

Despite all their altered testimony, not one of the state's witnesses identified Joe Hill as the murderer at the end of the prosecution's case. In place of identification there were phrases like "looked alike," "about the same," "seemed to be the same," and "appears to be the same."

Coupled with this weakness was the prosecution's failure to prove that one of the gunmen had actually been wounded in Morrison's store. All that Merlin Morrison said was: "As father fell my brother turned around to the shelf by the icebox. . . . There was a revolver there, and he picked it up. He certainly was brave, for he ran to where the scales are and shot. I *think* the bullet hit one man."[16] But Merlin did not see Arling pick up his father's gun or see him shoot it. He heard no exclamations of pain and had no other reason to believe the gun had been fired.

In his report, Dr. McHugh had stated that the bullet that struck Joe Hill went clean through his body and continued on its course. But no slug from the gun was ever found in the grocery store, which was minutely searched both on the night of the slaying and many times thereafter, and none was produced at the trial. Thus if Arling Morrison did hit one of the gunmen, he fled with the slug in his body—and Joe Hill had no slug in his body when he was examined by Dr. McHugh. Nor was blood found in the grocery store in the area where the gunmen were standing during the attack, and there was none found in front of the store. To be sure, a trail of blood was traced from the sidewalk near the store. But the state's own expert at the trial, Chemist Harris, upon being shown samples of the blood which the police testified was scraped from the sidewalk (and which was "presumed to be the blood of one of the robbers who was wounded"), testified only that it was mammalian blood. He "declined to say whether it was human blood." When, on cross-examination, the defense sought to show that the blood might have been from a wounded dog, the state interrupted to say "that expert testimony would be used to show that the blood was of a human being."[17] But no such "expert testimony" was ever introduced!

Dr. McHugh was one of the last witnesses for the state. He repeated his earlier story that Hill came to his office for treatment for a gunshot wound. "He said . . . that he was as much to blame as the other man and he wished it kept a secret." Dr. McHugh removed the clothing from the upper part of Hill's body and dressed the wound. He identified a shirt, undershirt, and coat, which were a part of the state's exhibits, as those worn by Hill at the time.[18]

Before the trial, in a report to the police and in interviews with the press, Dr. McHugh had said that Joe Hill's wound was made by a gun of a caliber larger than .32.[19] At the trial he volunteered the opinion that "the caliber of the gun, as evidenced by the size of the wound, I should judge to be of larger caliber than .32, and somewhere from .38 to .40 or .41." The bullets from Arling Morrison's gun were .38 caliber, and the prosecutor was allowed, over the defense's objection, to lead the witness to say that there was a "general resemblance" between Hill's wound and a .38-caliber wound. "The witness," the defense protested, "has shown no previous acquaintance with firearms and yet passes upon the size of the gun that made the wound."[20]

Since both Morrison and his son were killed with bullets fired from a .38-caliber automatic pistol,[21] the state tried to give the impression, through Dr. McHugh's testimony, that this was the same gun he had seen fall from Hill's clothing when his wound was being dressed. But on cross-examination, Dr. McHugh was shown an automatic Colt and an automatic Luger, and he was unable to say which one resembled the gun that fell from Hill's clothes in his office.[22]

HILL DISMISSES HIS LAWYERS

About halfway through the state's presentation of its case, Joe Hill created a "sensation"[23] by stopping the proceedings and demanding that his attorneys be discharged. Hill had been thinking of such a step as soon as the defense counsel cross-examined Merlin

Morrison. Even reporters noted that instead of questioning the boy vigorously, defense counsel merely went over with him the testimony he had given during the direct examination.[24] F. B. Scott, in a letter to the Salt Lake *Telegram* in August 1915, conceded that he and McDougall had cross-examined Merlin "gently," and explained: "We were afraid that any vigor in cross-examination would make the little boy cry and we well know what effect this would have on the jury." Scott also argued that "the boy did not attempt to identify Hillstrom as one of the men (in the store). Then why should we attempt to shake the little fellow's testimony?" Scott's first point has substance. Reports of Merlin Morrison's direct testimony described him as speaking "with eyes filled with tears. . . . It was with considerable effort that the lad restrained himself from breaking down."[25] Although Joe Hill felt that "vigor in cross-examination" was required, it seems obvious that such an approach would have caused the boy, who had seen his father and brother killed before his eyes, to have broken down. The effect of this on the jury would have been disastrous for the defendant. It is difficult to see how anything but a gentle and patient approach in cross-examination of Merlin Morrison could have been followed in Joe Hill's own interest.*

Scott's second point, however, is less convincing. Merlin Morrison *did* "attempt to identify" Joe Hill, but was unable to do so. If no attempt had been made, his testimony—the key to the entire case— would have been pointless. All of the Salt Lake City newspapers commented for several days after the murders that Merlin Morrison kept changing his story. Counsel for the defense should have taken advantage of this and conducted a more thorough cross-examination, even if a gentle and patient one.

Hill was also dismayed by the failure of defense counsel to use the records of the preliminary hearing, "and pin the witness[es] down to their former statements." With the disappearance of the transcript of the hearing, it is impossible to track down the exact discrepancy between what the state's witnesses said there and what they said at the trial. But we have already mentioned a number of

---

* In his article, "Some Gentle Hints on the Art of Cross-Examination," Leo R. Friedman, California attorney, writes: "On cross-examination never browbeat an elderly person or a young child. . . . Members of the American public and, therefore, jurors, resent such tactics." (*Case and Comment,* Jan. 1964, p. 10.)

such discrepancies, and it would have been logical for defense counsel to vigorously pursue the course Hill pointed out.

At any rate, on June 19, during Mrs. Seeley's testimony, Joe Hill arose and asked if he could speak. His request was granted. "I have three prosecuting attorneys here," he said (meaning the prosecuting attorney plus the two defense attorneys), "and I intend to get rid of two of them. Mr. Scott and Mr. McDougall, do you see that door? Get out of that door. I am through with you." After discharging his attorneys, Hill announced that he would handle his own case, that he wanted to recall the state's witnesses and cross-examine them himself. "I will prove that I was not at the Morrison grocery store that night. You can bring buckets of blood if you like, but you can't fool me." The bailiff forced Hill to take his seat, and his discharged counsel was directed to proceed with the cross-examination of Mrs. Phoebe Seeley. When Hill interrupted and ordered Scott out of the room, the attorney replied that he was present "by order of the court." "But can't I discharge my own attorneys?" Hill demanded. "You can," replied Judge Ritchie, "but I have asked the attorneys to stay here for a while as friends of the court, and they will cross-examine the witnesses just as before. You may take part in the proceedings."[26]

A large part of the argument between Joe Hill and his attorneys and the Judge was conducted in the presence of the jury. The jury, it is clear, should have been excused immediately.

The trial moved ahead, with Joe Hill still represented by two attorneys in whom he had lost confidence.* Judge Orrin Nelson Hilton of Denver, the distinguished attorney for the Western Federation of Miners, was persuaded to come to Joe Hill's legal defense. Hilton had been approached by Mrs. Virginia Snow Stephen, art instructor at the University of Utah and daughter of a former Mormon Church President. While on vacation in Denver, Mrs. Stephen urged Hilton to aid in Hill's defense. (Asked by the Salt Lake *Tribune* why, though she had never seen Hill, she had "become so firmly convinced of his innocence," she replied: "The man who wrote the songs and composed the music that Joseph Hillstrom has simply could not be guilty of so brutal a murder as the killing of the Morrisons.") Hilton was unable to conduct the defense at the time, but retained Soren X. Christensen, a Salt Lake City

* The court erred in appointing counsel without having been requested to do so and in forcing attorneys on a defendant not desiring them. (*See* Korf v. Jasper County, 132, Iowa 682, 108 N.W. 1031, 1907.)

attorney, to become his associate in the case. On the very day Hill dismissed Scott and McDougall, Mrs. Stephen sent a telegram to Christensen in Salt Lake City: "Sit in Hillstrom case now on trial in Ritchie court saving all exceptions possible with view of taking to supreme court. Judge Hilton makes this request."[27] Evidently Judge Hilton felt that the damage had already been done by the failure of the defense attorneys to cross-examine the state's witnesses effectively.

Christensen was not familiar with the case and probably convinced Hill that he would be better off with the experience of his former attorneys. Moreover, Christensen wanted payment for his services and no arrangement had yet been made for this. Thus Hill had no choice but to re-engage Scott and McDougall for the remainder of the trial. Shortly, however, Christensen joined Hill's defense. He had received a wire from Hilton telling him that their fee would be paid by the Denver local of the I.W.W. "I take it from the telegram," Christensen declared, "that Judge Hilton is engaged as counsel in the case too, though I do not expect him to come to Salt Lake for the present. . . . He probably has been engaged with a view to fighting the case further in case of a conviction."[28] This proved to be an accurate prediction. Hilton did not participate in the case until it was argued before the Supreme Court of Utah more than a year later.

Testimony for the state ended on the afternoon of June 23, and the defense immediately moved for a directed verdict of not guilty, charging insufficient evidence. The court overruled the motion and the defense thereupon presented its case.[29]

THE DEFENSE'S CASE

The defense set out to prove:

(1) That other men answering the general description of Hill had been and were still under suspicion of having committed the murder.

(2) That Hill was shot with a steel bullet and not with a lead bullet.

(3) That Hill could not have been shot in Morrison's store by Arling Morrison.

(4) That if any man was shot in Morrison's store that night, of which there was a grave doubt, he carried the bullet from the store

in his body, whereas the bullet with which Hill was shot went cleanly through his body and was not carried away by him.

(5) That the gun which Hill had on him when examined by Dr. McHugh was not a gun which could shoot the kind of bullets introduced in evidence as found in Morrison's store.

(6) That undue influence was used in attempting to get Hill to confess a crime he never committed; that witnesses subpoenaed by the defense had been approached by the state in an effort to get them to change their testimony so as to favor the state's case; and that witnesses for the state "altered their testimony from the time they were first examined at the preliminary hearing in order to make the facts fit Mr. Hillstrom in this case."[30]

But the defense was seriously hampered in establishing these points by Judge Ritchie's rulings refusing to allow witnesses to testify on issues that were crucial for the defendant. The court sustained objections by the prosecution to the introduction of evidence relevant to the arrest of other suspects and the belief at the time of the murder that certain of Morrison's neighbors were implicated in his death.[31] The court refused to allow a witness to prove that the police used unfair methods to make a case against Hill; refused to permit Hardy Downing, a newspaper reporter, to testify that Morrison had told him that the purpose of a previous holdup in his store "was not to rob him but kill him," and that he feared that the men would return; refused to allow the defense to prove that one of the men picked up as a suspect after the killings and subsequently released had had blood upon him when apprehended by the police, and dismissed defense attorney's argument that "other men have been held and turned loose, and we desire to know why."[32] The court refused to permit Dr. M. F. Beer, an expert medical witness, to answer a question that was essential to the defense. The bullet with which Joe Hill was shot pierced the left lung and exited under a shoulder blade. But the bullet holes in his coat, front and back, were four inches lower than the wounds. The defense contended he was shot while his hands were in the air and while he was facing his assailant. At no time were either of the two gunmen in this position, according to Merlin Morrison. The defense asked Dr. Beer the question:

"Q. And did you find that when his hands were raised extreme length over his head, and he was in an erect position, as to whether then the hole in the coat exactly corresponded with the wound in the body?

A. It does."

But the following question was never answered:

"Q. Would you then say, Doctor, that it was impossible for a bullet to have struck him with his arms in any other position than directly over his head, and himself in a perpendicular position?"

An objection was raised by Leatherwood, and Judge Ritchie ruled against the question.[33] Yet the fact that Joe Hill had been shot on the night the murders occurred was the only reason he had been arrested in the first place and later charged with murder. With the failure of any of the witnesses to identify Hill as one of the men in the store, this type of evidence became doubly important. But the Judge, who had no hesitations about helping a state witness come close to identifying Hill, refused to permit the admission of testimony essential for the defense.

E. J. Miller of the Western Arms & Sporting Goods Co., a man with 14 years' experience in handling guns, was the special target of prejudicial court rulings because he was the principal defense witness.

Miller testified that the empty shell in the revolver found by the dead body of Arling Morrison had been loaded with smokeless or semi-smokeless powder; hence no one could tell with any degree of accuracy how long ago the gun had been fired. The state's witnesses—none an expert—had testified that when they found the gun, they were convinced that it had been just discharged. Even though the witness was, and had for several years been, a salesman for a leading gun company, with long experience in handling and regularly testing makes and types of guns and ammunition, the court ruled out much of his testimony on the ground that he was not an expert.

Miller also testified that the wound in Hill's body was caused by a steel-jacketed bullet, whereas the man who was shot in the Morrison store was wounded with a lead bullet. He explained that he had examined the wound scars on Hill's body and concluded that the bullet "keyholed" in passing through Hill's body, that it turned slightly, thus causing a larger exit hole than the entrance. Lead bullets cause larger exit holes than steel bullets. Miller also declared that a lead bullet, especially a soft lead bullet, leaves a black lead mark when it makes a wound, and that steel bullets do not. Hill's body bore no lead mark. The state objected to this testimony, and was upheld by the court, who instructed the jury to ignore it. In doing so, Judge Ritchie ruled that Miller "has no medical knowledge, and therefore he cannot give an opinion," and then proceeded to usurp the role of a medical expert himself by stating flatly that the healing of Hill's wound rendered any discussion of the subject incompetent.[34]

A reading of the existing trial record clearly indicates that the court erred in favor of the prosecution in permitting Leatherwood too broad a latitude in cross-examination of defense witnesses, even permitting examination of matters not introduced by the defense.[35] A good example of the court's partisanship occurred during the testimony of a defense witness who, in response to a question from Leatherwood, hesitated momentarily. The following conversation took place:

"Q. Why did you hesitate?

Mr. McDougall: Hesitate what?

Mr. Leatherwood: I asked the witness why he hesitated.

Mr. Christensen: I shall object to the last question because there is no evidence he did hesitate. Let's get the record straight.

Mr. Leatherwood: We will let the jury determine that Mr. Christensen.

The Court: Gentlemen; you are making a record. The jury saw what he actually did, whether he hesitated or not. They will judge; so far as the record is concerned, that probably cannot be transferred from their minds to the record. . . .

Mr. Christensen: I would like a ruling on that question so I don't forget it. He asked why he hesitated. I object to it as incompetent, irrelevant and immaterial.

The Court: You want me to rule in the presence of the jury? I shall have to tell what I think about it. My own recollection is—of course the jury will not be influenced by this—my own recollection is that the witness did hesitate."[36]

But Christensen had not asked for a personal judgement, and certainly Judge Ritchie knew this. He wanted a statement of law which would nullify or admit the hesitation of any witness as a relevant consideration for the jury. He did not ask whether the witness had hesitated.

Despite the severe limitations imposed upon it by the court, the defense was able to establish a number of significant points. The state had made much of the fact that the red bandana handkerchief found in Hill's room at the Eselius house was exactly like the handkerchief worn over the face of one of the killers. But Mrs. Betty Eselius Olsen, testifying for the defense, stated that the faded red handkerchief taken from the table near Hill's bed belonged to her, that she had given it to him the Sunday morning *after* he was shot, and that he had not had this or a similar handkerchief on Saturday night. Her story stood up under cross-examination.[37] With all the restrictions placed upon his testimony by the court, Miller could hardly get his main points clearly across to the jury. But he did make it clear that Hill was not shot by the gun in Morrison's store.

There were several points defense counsel could have made and failed to do. It might have demonstrated how unlikely it was for a man to walk more than five miles on a winter's night with a wound such as Joe Hill had received. If his wound was received at about 9:45, could he have lasted more than two hours, or would he more likely have collapsed from loss of blood? This question had puzzled reporters when Hill was arrested,[38] yet it was not raised at the trial. Defense counsel could have pointed out that when Hill appeared at Dr. McHugh's office, the coat he wore "was soaked with blood, which was spurting from the wound"—in other words, a wound that was fresh, and not one two hours old which would by then have hardened and caked on his clothes.[39] It might have also been pointed out that Joe Hill did not hide after he was shot, but went to a doctor whom he had previously visited and thus knew him and could easily identify his patient.

Joe Hill claimed that prior to the murder of Morrison he had purchased a Luger pistol with a smaller caliber than the .38-caliber automatic gun used in the killing of the grocer and his son. This was the gun he had with him when he was examined by Dr. Mc-Hugh and which he discarded on the trip to Murray. Four days before his trial opened, Hill went with detectives to the pawnshop where he had purchased the gun. The records of the shop showed that he had purchased a gun there on December 15, 1913, but the caliber and make were not specified. "Hillstrom was crestfallen at his failure but he declared that he would prove that he had a gun . . . of smaller caliber," the Salt Lake *Tribune* reported.[40] Learning that the clerk who sold him the gun was in Chicago, Hill had a telegram sent to him. This brought the answer: "Remember selling Luger gun at that time. What's the trouble?"[41] Yet this all-important witness was not brought back by the defense to testify. Reporter Rae Wellman posed this very question in the Salt Lake *Telegram*:

"*Is that gun the gun?* Is the gun his? Were the cartridges and the bullets from that particular gun? . . .

"What was the caliber of Hill's revolver?

"Why didn't they call the pawnshop clerk who wired from Chicago?"[42]

The defense closed its case without Joe Hill testifying. He had repeatedly explained he had received his wound in a quarrel over a woman. On the eve of the trial the Salt Lake *Tribune* reported: "He refuses to disclose the name of the woman, declaring that he will go to his death rather than bring her name to light."[43] He was interrogated many times on this point, and never contradicted himself. Hill's refusal to testify thus came as no surprise to the Salt Lake City press.

CLOSING ARGUMENTS

E. D. McDougall made the opening argument for the defense. He began with a vigorous attack on criminal procedure. Under the law, he pointed out, the accused person is deemed innocent until proved guilty, but in practice the police and prosecuting attorneys treat accusation and guilt synonymously. After this introduction, McDougall turned to the specific case of Joe Hill. He branded Mrs. Seeley's testimony a "frame-up" executed by the prosecution. She lied when she testified that she noticed a defect on the neck of the tall man and that the defect was similar to a scar on Hill's neck. She lied in her statements regarding the general resemblance between Hill and one of the two men she said she saw in the vicinity of the Morrison store on the night of the murder. Merlin, he emphasized, was the only one who saw the murder, and he did not identify Hill. Moreover, there was no proof that Arling had shot at anyone. Even granting that he did and that the shot was effective, the man wounded could not have been Hill. The relative position of the persons in the store and the fact that Hill must have been shot with his hands in the air, precluded that possibility. "About the only thing we are sure of in this case is that the man in the Morrison store had a red handkerchief around his face and when he was on the street the handkerchief was around his neck. The evidence shows that the red handkerchief introduced by the state belonged to the Eselius household. It was given to Hillstrom by Mrs. Eselius on the Sunday morning following the holdup of the store and the murder of the Morrisons. The wound in Hillstrom's body is 4 feet and 2 inches from the bottom of his feet. The relative positions of the persons in the store as described by witnesses were such as to prove that Hillstrom was not the man shot by Arling Morrison, if indeed, one was shot."

McDougall concluded by telling the jury he did not know why Hill refused to tell how he was shot. "I do not know how he was shot, but I know that he was not shot in the Morrison store. But his refusal to tell where or how he was wounded should not be held against him. It is not the duty of the defendant to prove that he is innocent; the burden is on the state to prove that the defendant is guilty." Reminding the jury that the entire case against Hill was based on circumstantial evidence, he argued that "the state's evidence must form a complete chain, that a chain is only as strong as its weakest link, and that if the state had failed to complete a single link, the jury must find the defendant not guilty."[44]

Soren X. Christensen spoke next. He also reviewed the testimony of Mrs. Seeley, and pointed out that while she saw some similarities between Hill and the tall man, she would not say that the man was Hillstrom. Just the same he charged her with lying, and alluded to a "fix." If she had told the truth, uninfluenced by the prosecution, then why had Leatherwood not examined her husband, who also saw a tall and a short man walking near the store? Because, he declared, Mr. Seeley would have offered contrary evidence. Christensen also noted that if Arling Morrison had shot someone that man could not have been Hill, for the bullet that wounded Hill went clear through his body, and the man Arling was supposed to have shot must have carried it away with him in his body.

Finally, he stressed the lack of a motive for the killing as "the weak point in the State's case," for men did not kill without a motive, and the state had failed to show in any way that Joe Hill had a motive for the murder he was charged with. At first he had thought that robbery was the motive for the crime, but on becoming better acquainted with the case, he found he was mistaken. "There is not one line of evidence in the record here to show robbery as the motive. No attempt was made to rob the store, no word of robbery was spoken. No one was asked to throw up his hands. The murderers merely exclaimed to Morrison, 'We've got you now,' and then began shooting." But there must have been a motive to send these men into the store? Yet there was no evidence showing that Hill even knew Morrison. "Their lives had never crossed. Surely he had no reason for killing him. Remember that, gentlemen, when you retire to the jury room. Unless you find a motive, and you cannot since none was shown by the state, you must acquit this man."[45]

F. B. Scott's address to the jury received little attention in the press. All we know is that he reviewed the evidence in the case step by step, declaring that he could not understand how a jury could find the defendant guilty.[46]

In his closing argument, prosecutor Leatherwood stooped to the lowest possible level to sway the jury to deliver a verdict of guilty, and he did not hesitate to drive home by clear implication that Joe Hill's I.W.W. membership was enough to justify such a verdict. Leatherwood described the murder of Arling in graphic detail, and declared that the hand of fate had intervened and left an indelible stamp of guilt on the fiend who shot him:

"Ah, it was a cruel thing, the killing of the child. And not content with rendering him helpless, one of the brutes deliberately . . . leaned over the counter and fired thrice into the boy's body to make sure no spark of his childish life should remain."

The "fiend" who did that deed was not "some monstrous cyclops but rather some cool thing, some bloodless thing, some thing in which the springs of humanity had been stopped up, *some thing in which runs the acid of hate*. That is the kind of thing that could kill that boy." There is no question that Leatherwood was reminding the jury that the I.W.W., as usually pictured in the press, was an organization whose philosophy was based on hate of capitalism.

When he had thus pictured the murderer, Leatherwood turned abruptly toward Hill, pointed an accusing finger at him, and thundered:

"That man was Hillstrom . . . and the bullet fired by that boy just before he too fell under the fire of the cowardly brutes, penetrated the breast of the murderer and by that token the law has sought him out. Murder will come out and I tell you it speaks louder than a voice from a mountain top."

It was not the facts of the case which convinced Leatherwood of Hill's guilt, but the defendant's failure to testify and explain his wound:

"Joseph Hillstrom, if you were an innocent man, you would have told how you received that wound. Why in God's name did you not tell, so that your name could have been cleared from the stain upon it? Because you did not dare, Joe Hillstrom! Because you could not tell a story that could have been corroborated. That is why?"

Leatherwood fiercely attacked Defense Attorney McDougall, accusing him of deception and lack of patriotism. How did he dare to attack criminal procedure? His blood boiled with resentment when he heard such unwarranted attacks on American institutions, "institutions which are the foundation stones of our glorious concepts of liberty, equality and justice." When "any considerable number of our fellow beings," he continued, "subscribe to the doctrine you heard enunciated here this morning, then liberty flees the confines of our fair land and *anarchy* begins the sway." After thus reminding the jury that the defendant was a member of an organization accused of favoring anarchy, Leatherwood climaxed his appeal with words which could not fail to impress the jury that Joe Hill was no ordinary man but a prominent Wobbly:

". . . enforce the majesty of the law as framed by the people of this great state; enforce it so that *anarchy and murder and crime* shall be pushed back beyond the pole of civilization; enforce it so that you and your sons and all upright men shall walk the earth free from the danger of those *parasites on society who murder and rob rather than make an honest living.*"[47]

Is there any doubt that Leatherwood was painting the general public conception of the I.W.W. "The current picture," wrote Paul F. Brissenden in 1918 in his book, *The I.W.W.,* "is of a motley horde of hoboes . . . who will not work and whose philosophy is a philosophy simply of *sabotage* and the violent overthrow of 'capitalism' and whose actions conform to that philosophy . . . they are arch-fiends and the dregs of society."[48]

The day after Leatherwood's closing argument, Scott took exception to the prosecutor's remarks "upon the subject of the silence of the defendant or his refusal to make any explanation or to take the witness stand in his own behalf."[49] The objection was well-taken: Utah law provides that the defendant's "neglect or refusal to be a witness shall not in any manner prejudice him, nor be used against him in the trial, or proceeding."[50] Even though the speech to the jury as reported in the press included the remarks objected to, Leatherwood vigorously denied having made the statement. He felt safe, for his words had not been recorded in the trial record, and he knew that for that reason the defense would not be able to assign the error when the case was later appealed.[51]

The defense failed to point out other errors in Leatherwood's address to the jury, either because they failed to recognize them or because they realized that it was pointless to do so, since no record was made. For one thing, the general tone of Leatherwood's argument was highly inflammatory, calculated to stir the emotions of the jury and excite prejudice against the defendant. At that time, many courts had declared such practices constituted grounds for reversal.[52] Leatherwood's references to the character of the defendant might also have been objected to. He denounced Hill as a brute, fiend, parasite on society, an instigator of anarchy, and a maker of "widows and orphans." Less abusive language than this had secured freedom for men convicted long before Hill, especially when no evidence substantiating the charges were included in the trial record and there was not a clear case of guilt.[53] Finally, much of what Leatherwood said was totally irrelevant, pertaining to the murder of Arling and not his father, and Hill was not on trial for the slaying of the son. Certainly, too, the indirect references to Hill's affiliation with the I.W.W. were completely irrelevant. At that time, many courts had declared such practices constituted ground for reversal.[54]

JUDGE'S INSTRUCTIONS TO JURY

The trial came to a close with Judge Ritchie's instructions to the jury. He first instructed the jury that they must find beyond a reasonable doubt that the defendant, according to the information, had unlawfully, wilfully, deliberately, maliciously, premeditatedly, and with specific intent, taken the life of J. G. Morrison. Such a finding would enable them to return a verdict of first degree murder. Lesser offenses, second degree murder and manslaughter, could, however, be found under the same information. He proceeded to define reasonable doubt, aiding and abetting, circumstantial evidence, and suspicion. Other instructions mentioned presumption of innocence, the right of the accused to refrain from testifying, the presence or absence of motive, false testimony, and the credibility of witnesses. He dismissed the emphasis placed by defense counsel on the "absence of motive," but conceded that it was "a factor for the consideration of the jury." He instructed the jury that they were "bound to presume the defendant innocent until he is proven guilty beyond a reasonable doubt. . . . A defendant has a right, if he chooses so to do, to refrain from testifying in his own behalf . . . and you are instructed that you must not take into consideration, or in any manner be influenced by the fact that the defendant did not testify in this case."[55]

All this was preliminary to what had been most eagerly awaited —how Judge Ritchie would define circumstantial evidence. It was generally agreed that the jury's verdict as to the guilt or innocence of Joe Hill would be greatly influenced by the court's theory. Judge Ritchie could liken such evidence to a chain, each link or circumstance succeeding and depending upon the other, and if any link were not proven beyond a reasonable doubt, the chain would be destroyed and acquittal mandatory. This represented the position of the defense. Or, he might argue that circumstantial evidence was of the nature of a cable, that one or more strands could be broken and a cable, strong enough to support conviction, would remain. This was the position of the prosecution.

Judge Ritchie took the latter position:

"This kind of evidence is the proof of such facts and circumstances connected with or surrounding the perpetration of the crime charged, as to tend to show the guilt or innocence of the person accused; and if these facts and circumstances when considered all together, are sufficient to satisfy the mind of the jury of the guilt of the defendant beyond a reasonable doubt, then such evidence is sufficient to authorize a conviction. But if such facts and circumstances, when considered together, are explainable upon any other reasonable hypothesis than the defendant is guilty, then such evidence will not warrant a verdict of guilty."

Judge Ritchie vigorously disputed defense counsel's statement on the nature of circumstantial evidence that "each link must be proven beyond a reasonable doubt," emphasizing that "one weak strand or thread in the ends of circumstantial evidence did not necessarily cause the case built thereupon to collapse."[56] As James O. Morris points out, if Judge Ritchie's instructions had followed the defense's theory of circumstantial evidence, "the jury would have been morally and logically bound to return a verdict of not guilty."[57]

It is significant that Utah cases up to this time unanimously uphold the position taken by the defense. In 1894, the Supreme Court ruled it "incumbent upon the prosecution not only to show by a preponderance of evidence that an offense was committed . . . but that the alleged facts and circumstances are true. . . . The chain of circumstances must be complete and unbroken." Two years later, the opinion was repeated. "The chain of evidence must be complete and unbroken and established beyond a reasonable doubt." And again in 1898, when the matter was thoroughly considered, the court concluded that "when circumstances which succeed and depend upon each other as a chain alone are relied on for conviction, each link must be proved beyond a reasonable doubt."[58] The instruction asked for by the defense was thus based on clear precedent. In the trial of Joe Hill, there was no pretension of having direct evidence —and there was none. Had Judge Ritchie's instruction on circumstantial evidence been based on Utah precedent, Joe Hill would most likely have been declared innocent.

THE VERDICT

The case was given to the jury at 4:45 P.M., June 26. Having failed to reach a verdict by 11 o'clock, the jury was locked up for the night. In the meantime there was widespread rumor that the I.W.W. would create violence in the courtroom in case of a conviction. The Salt Lake *Tribune* reported the "Sheriff is Watchful. Remains on guard lest IWW friends of accused make demonstration."[59] The sheriff stationed a cordon of deputies around the courtroom, which was crowded with spectators, many of them Wobblies eagerly awaiting the verdict. Hill was completely surrounded by deputies, and several stood in the corridor just outside the courtroom door.[60]

At 10 A.M., June 27, 1914, the jury announced its verdict. "We, the Jurors impaneled in the above case, find the defendant Joseph Hillstrom guilty of the crime of murder in the first degree as charged in the information." The jury made no recommendation for clemency. The Deseret *Evening News* felt cheated because Joe Hill had heard the verdict "without the flutter of an eye." "There was not even a change of color in his cheeks," its reporter lamented, and Hill had shown "less concern than many other times during his trial."[61]

The Salt Lake *Tribune* headlined the news, "First Degree Is Verdict," and commented: "Hillstrom is an I.W.W. . . . His songs and verses have been adopted by the national organization and are used as revolutionary songs."[62] A few days after the verdict, the paper noted: "The song book of the I.W.W., under the captions, 'Songs to Fan Flames of Discontent,' contains a total of thirteen songs by Hillstrom. All are parodies on either popular or sacred music and all are of an inflammatory nature and in keeping with the caption of the book quoted above."[63] The implication was clear throughout the article that guilty or not, Joe Hill was the type of man better removed from American society.

As Joe Hill left the courtroom following the verdict of the jury, he turned to the reporter of the Deseret *Evening News,* and, as the latter wrote, declared that "he was innocent of the killing and that he would prove it before he got through."[64]

HILL SENTENCED TO DEATH

Still heavily guarded, Hill was ushered into the same court on July 8 for the passing of sentence. At that time, Utah was the only state in the union conferring upon a prisoner facing execution the privilege of choice in the manner of death. Judge Ritchie informed his prisoner that he could die either by hanging or facing a firing squad. "I'll take the shooting," was the answer. "I'm used to that. I've been shot at a few times in the past, and I guess I can stand it, again." Ritchie then passed sentence:

"The judgment of this court is that you, Joseph Hillstrom, be committed and you are hereby committed to the custody of the warden of the state prison and that you be taken to the state prison and there kept by the warden until Sept. 4, 1914, and that on Sept. 4 within the exterior walls of the state prison between the hours of sunrise and sun-set you be shot until you are dead by the sheriff of Salt Lake County."[65]

At the same time, the court granted a motion by Christensen for a new trial and another staying the execution until argument for a new trial could be heard.

CHAPTER FOUR

The Defense Campaign

After the sentencing of Joe Hill the campaign in his behalf really got under way. For several months, Hill had refused to allow the I.W.W. to come to his aid, stubbornly insisting that the affair was a personal, not a union, concern. Money needed for organizational purposes should not be diverted for his defense, Joe Hill told the Salt Lake City I.W.W. leaders. He did, however, allow Ed Rowan to appeal for his defense on a personal basis to friends on the West Coast.[1] Evidently, very little came in; it will be recalled that Hill had no money to hire a lawyer and acted as his own attorney at the preliminary hearing.

Finally, in early April, Hill agreed that his case was of concern to the entire I.W.W. On April 18, 1914, *Solidarity* printed the first release on the case. It was an appeal to "Rally to Defense of Joe Hill. Man who wrote 'Mr. Block' and 'Casey Jones' caught and held on trumped-up charges." It also stated that he was being made the victim of a "conspiracy of the Utah Construction Company, the Utah Copper Company, and the Mormon Church," because he was a "thorn in the side of the master class." In *Solidarity* of May 23, Ed Rowan reported that about $200 had been received, and in order "to enlighten the membership," he gave the facts in the case. "The main thing the state has against Hill is that he is an I.W.W. and *therefore sure to be guilty.** For this reason he is entitled to be helped and not allowed to hang for being an I.W.W." In the same issue there was an announcement that a Joe Hill Defense Committee had been elected by the Salt Lake City locals, and "every fellow worker who has sung any of Hill's songs ought to contribute, if it is only a dime."[2]

Salt Lake City papers carried news of the activities of the Defense Committee. On June 20, the *Tribune* reported the attendance at the trial of "a large number of men who are said to be associated with the Industrial Workers of the World." It also reported that the Defense Committee had worked with Mrs. Virginia Snow Stephens in

---

* This is an actual quotation, word for word, from a letter sent by Hill's attorneys, Scott and McDougall. *See* reference notes, chapter IV, note 7.

persuading Judge Hilton to come into the case. On June 27, *Solidarity* carried a dispatch from Ed Rowan, reporting that the trial was "now on in full blast." The article disclosed that the Defense Committee was having difficulty in raising funds because many were asking, "If Fellow Worker Joe Hill is innocent, why does he not state specifically where he was that particular evening of January 10, 1914?" Rowan replied sharply:

"We recognize the fact that Hill was not arrested in connection with labor troubles, and that he has remained silent as to his movements the night of said murder. On the other hand, Hill has devoted what talent he possessed to the cause of labor, he never asked the organization at any time to help save him from conviction. But now that the organization has taken it up all over, we must stand by him to the last ditch, as we cannot afford to lose a rebel of his calibre and ability, no matter whether the powers deem him guilty or not. The laws of this great and glorious country state on paper (not in action) that any accused member of society is presumed to be innocent till proven guilty. In practice though it works out different, seemingly, as now Fellow Worker Hill starts out guilty, and is expected to prove his innocence against prejudice of the deepest kind.

"Well, here is the stand of the rebels in Salt Lake City, we say to hell with that brand of bunk, and having no other course to pursue, we call upon all workers to ditch every speck of capitalistic morals or ethics concealed in their cranium, and come to front strong with all the financial support they can muster toward fighting this case. If you have not been heard from so far do your best and forward all you can raise or spare to Geo. Child, Treasurer Hill Defense, 118 W. S. Temple Street, Salt Lake City."

Two weeks later, Rowan reported the verdict of the jury, and stated that since the Salt Lake rebels had had a premonition of such an outcome despite the lack of evidence presented by the state, they had retained Judge Hilton to carry the case higher, if necessary. They still had "the greatest faith and belief in Hill," and were prepared to appeal for a new trial once the funds were provided. But would the many thousands who knew Joe Hill through his songs remain silent and do nothing? If so, "Fellow Worker Hill is lost."[3]

The I.W.W. came through. "Shall Joe Hill Be Murdered?" asked Haywood in *Solidarity*, July 25, 1914. Noting that Hill was convicted "on the flimsiest kind of circumstantial evidence," he appealed to all Wobblies and their friends to write to Governor Spry and the prosecuting attorney demanding a new trial, and, at the same time, to send money to the Hill Defense Fund in Salt Lake City.

MASS PROTESTS

The response to Haywood's appeal put the Utah authorities on notice for the first time that they were dealing with more than a local issue. Letters and telegrams began pouring into the offices of Governor Spry and the district and county attorneys, demanding a new trial or a pardon. They came from a mass meeting of 500 workers in Tacoma, Washington, the Women's Christian Temperance Union of California, the Tonapah Miners' Union and the Tonapah local of the Socialist Party, and scores of individuals, non-I.W.W. members as well as those belonging to the organization. "I am not an I.W.W.," wrote E. E. Hahn of Yale, Oklahoma, "but have been watching Joe Hill's trial and can see no justice in murdering a man on circumstantial evidence. . . . If Hill is killed . . . it will make 10,000 new I.W.W. . . . I will join the I.W.W. myself." Hahn, who described himself as an "oil magnate," promised to "donate $50,000 to the labor cause" if Joe Hill was executed in spite of a trial which was a "farce."[4]

The Deseret *Evening News,* obviously astonished by the volume of protest, editorially reminded the protestants that they lived out of the state and were, therefore, dependent for their information about the trial on brief newspaper reports. It conceded, however, that a "mistake" might have been made in this case—the only time any Salt Lake City newspaper conceded there might have been a "mistake" in the verdict—but since the jury had found Joe Hill guilty, the likelihood was that he had committed the offense with which he was charged. Of one thing it was certain: "There was no more effort to convict him on the part of our prosecuting officials than is made in any other case. And there was no excitement on the part of the public. That the condemned man was a member of the I.W.W. should make no difference in the case."[5] The editorial writer, however, ignored the fact that the police and the Deseret *Evening News,* like all the other Salt Lake City newspapers, had found Joe Hill guilty even before the trial, and had helped create a hostile atmosphere against him, prejudicing potential members of the jury by picturing him as an experienced, hardened criminal, and a revolutionary agitator to boot.

Letters and telegrams continued to pour into Salt Lake City. Late in August, the Salt Lake *Tribune* reported, "Protests against the execution of Hillstrom have come from members of the IWW from all parts of the United States."[6] The national office of the I.W.W. tied in the case with the song book Joe Hill had helped make famous. "Special Feature for Publicity on Joe Hill Case," read the headline in *Solidarity* of August 29, 1914, and there followed the announcement: "After August 29th all orders for Song Books will be sent out accompanied with an equal number of folders the proper size for inserting in the books explaining the case of Fellow Worker Joe Hill, and urging the necessary action to prevent his being shot by the authorities of Salt Lake City. In this way the songs, of which he has contributed so many, will be a medium of arousing the workers in his behalf." Thousands of these leaflets were distributed. In addition, a Special "Joe Hill Edition" of the I.W.W. Song Book was issued; it included a printed insert "explaining the outrage and calling for action on the part of every purchaser of a copy of the songs."[7]

The first protest of an international nature in Hill's behalf came from London. On December 19, 1914, a meeting was held under the auspices of the British I.W.W. which passed a resolution "joining with the fellow workers of America in demanding the unconditional release of Joe Hill."[8] Shortly after, on January 2, 1915, the first notice of the interest in the case was received by the federal government. It was in the form of a letter to President Wilson enclosing a resolution adopted by the Trades Council and Local 644 U.M.W. of Hillboro, Illinois, complaining of unfairness in the trial of Joe Hill and advocating that the Governor and Attorney General of Utah act promptly in securing "a new and fair trial." "Our sending it," wrote Harry Brown, Secretary of the Trades Council and U.M.W. local, "is for the purpose of calling the President's attention to the case."[9]

Early in May 1915, during a cross-country speaking tour, Elizabeth Gurley Flynn visited Joe Hill in his cell. Although she had never met the I.W.W. troubadour, she had already spoken in his behalf and helped raise money for the defense fund and, beginning with January 1915, had started, at Hill's initiative, a steady correspondence with him.[10] Her story of the one-hour interview was published on the front page of *Solidarity* (May 22, 1915) under the headline: "A Visit to Joe Hill. I.W.W. Song Writer and Rebel

Shows Undaunted Spirit in Jail. $300 Needed At Once For Defense." The article closed:

"Joe Hill didn't ask the IWW to fight for him; he was in jail months before he'd consent to the locals' taking up his case. So the appeal is not for him, but in the spirit:

"'He's in their dungeon, dark and grim.

He stood by us, we'll stand by him!'

". . . Letters and telegrams to Gov. Spry will help, but money is the prime necessity.

"I appeal to you—help Joe Hill to 'fan the flames of discontent,' to fight (and sing)—a little longer!"*

Elizabeth Gurley Flynn's story, notes Barrie Stavis, "touched off a forward energetic movement in the continuing fight to save Joe Hill."[11] Funds came in sufficient amount to carry on the struggle. What one student has called "perhaps the most famous protest movement in American labor history"[12] was well under way.

While the case of Joe Hill was becoming famous throughout the United States and beginning to penetrate abroad, legal steps were under way to prevent the execution. After several delays, Christensen and Leatherwood presented their views for and against a new trial. Judge Ritchie heard both sides on September 1, 1914, and ruled on the issue the same day. Christensen mainly argued that Hill had not been identified as the slayer; that the only thing proved beyond a reasonable doubt was that he had been wounded on the night of the killing. Moreover, the discharge of defense attorneys and their retention as friends of the court, contrary to the wishes of Hill, had prejudiced the jury against him. Finally, the jurymen did not render their verdict impartially. When Christensen entered the case, he took one glance at the jury and "knew all hope was lost. . . . That jury was selected by a science at which the district attorney is a past master and the defendant's attorneys were unskilled." Leatherwood brushed these arguments aside, insisting that Hill was tried, convicted, and sentenced in strict accordance with the law, and ought to be executed without further delay. Judge Ritchie, as expected, agreed, and denied a new trial.[13]

* Miss Flynn was paraphrasing Joe Hill's parting remark to her: *"I'm not afraid of death, but I'd like to be in the fight a little longer."* (*Solidarity*, May 22, 1915.) Owing to the presence of the prison guard, Miss Flynn did not ask Joe Hill anything about the events leading to his arrest or any details of his case. (Interview with Elizabeth Gurley Flynn, Jan. 31, 1964.)

APPEAL TO UTAH SUPREME COURT

Christensen, not surprised by the decision, filed papers for an appeal to the Utah Supreme Court, automatically staying the execution a second time.

Judge Hilton and Soren Christensen completed legal preparations for the appeal in December, but the case was not decided until July 1915. The argument took place on May 28, 1915, Hilton and Christensen representing the appellant and Attorney General A. R. Barnes and Assistant Attorneys-General E. V. Higgins and G. A. Iverson the state.

In the brief submitted to the Supreme Court, the following arguments were advanced to justify the request that the higher court reverse the trial verdict and set aside the death sentence:

(1) Hill was denied his constitutional rights when police officials interrogated him in the absence of an attorney and subjected him to psychological coercion.

(2) Judge Ritchie erred prejudicially in allowing the admission of irrelevant testimony into evidence.

(3) Judge Ritchie erred in rejecting evidence in favor of the defendant.

(4) There was no evidence to support the verdict; no motive was shown and there was a failure of identification. The case should never have gone to the jury.

(5) Hill was denied due process and equal protection of the law because Judge Ritchie erred in his instruction to the trial jury on the nature of circumstantial evidence.

(6) Prosecutor Leatherwood tried to degrade Hill and inflame the jury against him and was also guilty of prejudicial conduct.

(7) Judge Ritchie prejudiced the jury against Hill by making unfavorable rulings against the defendant in the presence of the jury.

(8) Judge Ritchie erred in refusing to allow defense to ask questions to establish whether prospective jurymen were prejudiced against the defendant and in objecting to the time taken by defense to select jurymen.

(9) Judge Ritchie erred in asking the state witnesses leading questions.

(10) Judge Ritchie erred in allowing the defendant to continue his defense during the trial with no other counsel than the two attorneys he (the judge) appointed after the defendant made repeated attempts

to discharge counsel in accordance with his constitutional right.

The brief concluded:

"We feel that we have clearly shown that there is no identification of person; that no motive has been shown, and that in this case, under the testimony, motive is essential; that the testimony does not support the verdict, that the proceedings of the court on the *voir dire* of the jurors and leaving the defendant without counsel was error; and again on the instructions, which this court has so often and so clearly laid down as the proper instruction to follow, the trial court committed error. For these reasons, we respectfully suggest that manifest injustice has been done the defendant, requiring a reversal of conviction."[14]

Judge Hilton argued the appeal before the Supreme Court in person. He showed that the constitutional safeguards prescribed to assure a fair, impartial and unprejudiced trial had not been met. He argued further that because guilt had not been proved beyond a reasonable doubt, and because a motive had not been established, the court should be convinced that the verdict should not stand and the sentence be set aside. Merlin's testimony did not identify any particular person, and Phoebe Seeley had been encouraged by the prosecuting attorney to say things she would not have testified to voluntarily. Hilton contended further that the motive of Morrison's attackers appeared to have been revenge, yet no such motive had been proved to be connected in any way with Joe Hill. The only important court ruling he contested was the appointment by Judge Ritchie of Scott and McDougall as *amicae curiae* (friend of the court). The consequence of such action was to deny Hill the right to defend himself in person and to prejudice the jury against him. In conclusion, he said:

"I now ask your honors frankly, if you, or any one that is dear to you, was condemned upon the inconclusive, disjointed fragments of suspicion, misnomered by the state as evidence against this defendant, would you say that you or they were justly condemned and that the crime charged had been proved against you beyond a reasonable doubt?

"Would you, or would you permit anyone dear to you to go to his death under the flimsy testimony and then say that you or he had been tried, fairly and impartially, according to the laws of the land, and in accordance with the safeguards provided by the constitution?"[15]

"We are anxiously awaiting the verdict, and we hope to be able to wire *Solidarity* good news before long," Ed Rowan wrote optimistically at the end of the hearing before the Supreme Court. Hilton must have shared this optimism. On June 6, Hill wrote to Sam Murray, one of his companions in the rebel army during the 1911 revolution in Mexico: "My case was argued on the 28th of May, and according to Judge Hilton, the results were satisfactory. He says he is sure of securing a reversal, and if so, there hardly will be another trial, for the simple reason that there won't be anything to try."[16]

UTAH SUPREME COURT REJECTS APPEAL

The news came on July 3, but it was anything but good. Chief Justice D. N. Straup delivered the court's opinion affirming the trial verdict. Straup began by quoting at considerable length from Mrs. Seeley's testimony, placing great importance on the fact that she had brought out the similarity between the nose, thin face, scar and peculiar nostrils of the taller man and those of Joe Hill. He then noted that Merlin had witnessed the shooting of his father by a man who resembled Hill in general build and height. While Merlin did not see his brother fire the revolver, he had examined the gun before the two men had entered the store and found all six chambers loaded, whereas when the assailants withdrew, the gun was found with only five chambers loaded, one having been discharged. The logical inference, continued Chief Justice Straup, was "that at some time during the shooting Arling . . . got the gun, and discharged it at the assailants."[17]

Since the transcript of Merlin's testimony during the trial has disappeared, it is not possible to check this point in detail. But it is significant that Merlin's examination of the revolver prior to the entrance of the two men was not reported in the press, and it is difficult to understand how such important evidence would have been overlooked by the reporters. Since, as we shall see, there were many clear misstatements of facts in the Supreme Court opinion, it is possible to count this as one.

The court continued to review the elements of the case favorable to the state. Two witnesses saw the taller assailant "come out of the store in a rather stooped position, with his hands drawn over his chest" and the first witness "heard him exclaim as if in great pain, 'Oh, Bob!' and saw him cross the street to the alley." As he approached the alley, the second witness "heard him in a clear voice

say, 'I'm shot!'" The red bandana handkerchief found in Hill's
room was similar to those worn by the assailants. His coat and
clothing also were "similar in appearance to those worn by the taller
assailant."[18] The court ignored the fact that there were several ver-
sions of the type of clothing worn by the taller man, and only one
person, Dr. McHugh, had actually seen the clothes worn by Joe Hill
that night.

Dr. McHugh's testimony was completely falsified by the court.
Thus the court stated: "From the appearance of [Hill's] wound the
doctors [McHugh and Bird] gave it as their impression that the
bullet causing [it] was shot from a .38-caliber gun." But in the
reports of the testimony in the contemporary Salt Lake City press
and in the defense appeals brief, Dr. McHugh is quoted as testifying
regarding the caliber of the gun, as evidenced by the size of the
wound: "[I] should judge to be of large caliber, larger than .32,
and somewhere from .38 to .40 or .41." In short, he had refused to
make a definite commitment on the point, but the Supreme Court
made it for him. Again, referring to Hill's gun, the court stated
that "from the appearance of the handle they [Drs. McHugh and
Bird] gave it as their opinion that the gun was a .38-caliber gun, and
that the handle was similar to the Colt's automatic .38 gun exhibited
to them."[19] But Dr. McHugh had failed completely to identify Hill's
gun in any way whatever; he simply could not say whether Hill's
gun most resembled a Colt or a Luger. But the court said it for him:
it resembled a Colt automatic .38-caliber gun, which was the type
of weapon used to kill Morrison.

Probably the court falsified Dr. McHugh's testimony because the
justices realized that the state's evidence did not afford "substantial"
proof of guilt. The court admitted that Merlin's testimony, that in
general Hill resembled his father's attacker, was "alone not sufficient," and even that what was said by other witnesses who saw a
tall man running away from the store "also was insufficient." But,
the court continued:

"There is the further testimony of the witness [Mrs. Seeley] who
but a few minutes prior to the homicide . . . looked him [one of the
assailants]* directly in the face. . . . True, that witness would not
testify positively that the defendant was that man; but the facts
testified to by her as to the description of that man pointed most
strikingly to the defendant, and may be entitled to as much or more

* The court simply assumed that the person Mrs. Seeley had seen was one
of the assailants. She did not say he was.

weight than had the witness, without such description . . . testified that, in her opinion or judgment, the defendant was that man."[20]

It made no difference, therefore, that Merlin's testimony, delivered by the only person who had seen the murders, was "not sufficient," or that that of other witnesses was "also . . . insufficient." It even made no difference that Mrs. Seeley entertained an "honest doubt" that Joe Hill was the man. Even though Mrs. Seeley would not herself, as an eye-witness, conclude that Hill was the man, the court did it for her. Yet the court felt Mrs. Seeley's testimony still left it on insecure grounds in regard to basic identification, admitting that no one had adequately connected Hill with the murder. So, it fell back on what it called irrefutable proof that Hill was guilty: "the fresh bullet wound on the defendant."

"That wound, unexplained, or unsatisfactorily explained by him, was, in connection with other evidence that one of the perpetrators of the crime answering the defendant's description was shot in the store,* a relevant mark of identification . . . as much a distinguishing mark as though one of the assailants in the assault had one of his ears chopped off, or as though some stolen and identified article from the store had been found in his unexplained or unsatisfactorily explained possession."[21]

The court then regarded Hill's wound not only as a mere "relevant mark of identification" but as absolute proof of guilt. It simply assumed that he had been shot in the Morrison store, even though conceding that much of the evidence establishing this point was not convincing. It all boiled down to this: the court simply concluded that because Hill was proved to have been shot on the same night as the Morrison murders, he was guilty. And, after all, Joe Hill had refused to testify.

The court did not deny that Hill "had a right to remain silent and his neglect or refusal to be a witness" could not "in any manner prejudice or be used against him. The state, as in all other criminal cases, was required to prove the defendant's guilt beyond a reasonable doubt." But this was merely a general principle which the court refused to apply to the case under consideration. Otherwise, why did the judges call attention to the fact that:

"The defendant was not a witness in the case, and at no time explained or offered to explain the place where, nor the circumstances under which, he received his wound, except as stated by him to the

---

* The court is obviously basing this on Merlin's testimony, which, it had already declared, was "not sufficient."

doctors . . . nor did he offer any evidence whatever to show his
whereabouts or movements on the night of the homicide."[22]

Again, in concluding the argument on the identification of Hill
as the wanted criminal, the court declared that "the defendant, without some proof tending to refute them, may not avoid the natural
and reasonable inferences deducible from proven facts by merely
declining to take the stand or remaining silent."[23] But the court
had acknowledged that there was only one important fact proved—
that Hill was shot. Was it possible for an impartial court to draw
an inference of guilt from this fact as "natural and reasonable?"
The court was not impartial, however, and concluded that since
Hill would neither admit guilt nor clear himself, he must be considered guilty. Thus, for all the lip-service allegiance to the principle
that a defendant's refusal to testify could not "in any manner prejudice or be used against him," the court regarded Hill's failure to
testify as an actual admission of guilt.

The court dismissed the points raised by the appellant. As far as
motive was concerned, it did not have to be shown, even in a circumstantial case, in order to justify a finding of guilt. But the court did
not leave it at this: it supplied its own motive. It *knew* Hill intended
to murder or rob Morrison, and in either case "nothing but a wicked
motive emanating from a depraved and malignant heart is at-
tributable to the commission of such a crime as is here *indisputably*
shown."[24] So while motive was not required to prove guilt, the
court added one to justify its finding.

The only significant rule of the lower court involved in the appeal
was the appointment of defense counsel as *amicae curiae*. Speaking
for the whole court, Straup indicated that "though it should be
thought it [the] appointment was not proper," it had manifestly
redounded to the benefit of the defendant and not to his harm;
therefore while perhaps illegal, the action of the lower court was not
ground for a reversal.[25] The fact that Hill and many others felt that
the judge's action had deprived the defendant of adequate counsel
did not bother the Supreme Court.

Chief Justice Straup's two associates, justices J. E. Frick and
William M. McCarty, offered concurring opinions. McCarty believed that Hill was properly identified by Seeley, Mahan and Hansen, and he was particularly impressed by the latter's identification
of Hill's voice. He remembered her testimony that the voice of the
man she heard crying, "Oh, Bob!" was unusually clear and not at
all hoarse, and that Hill's voice sounded exactly the same. He

thereupon cited authority for the conclusive, incriminating nature of voice identification. But he conveniently overlooked the fact that the voice Mrs. Hansen heard was full of anguish and pain, and, in addition, uttered but two words. He also overlooked the fact that just two years before the Joe Hill case, the same Utah court dealt with the nature and validity of voice identification. The conclusion reached at that time is significant:

"While evidence of the sound of voice is admissible for identification purposes, it should be reasonably positive and certain, and based upon some *peculiarity of the voice or upon sufficient previous knowledge by the witness thereof.*"[26]

There was no question that Mrs. Hansen did not know Joe Hill and had no previous knowledge of his vocal quality or tone. Nor was the voice she heard "unusually clear." Certainly, then, there was nothing to justify the conclusion that the evidence was "reasonably positive and certain" that Hill's voice was the same one heard by Mrs. Hansen.

As he was to make clear later, McCarty was viciously opposed to the I.W.W. But even in his opinion he dropped a hint of his bias against the organization of which Hill was a leading member. He declared that the jury was justified in finding "the explanation the defendant gave of his wound was false, a mere subterfuge, and that *the Eselius home was at that time* [the time of the murder] *a rendezvous for criminals, and recognized as such by the defendant.*"[27]

No evidence covering this point had been introduced during the trial. It is, therefore, clear that Justice McCarty had in mind that Joe Hill was a Wobbly and that Applequist and several of the Eselius brothers, who worked with Hill in San Pedro, were probably also members of the I.W.W. His reference to "criminals" was simply another way of saying I.W.W.'s.

Justice Frick mainly concerned himself with Hill's alibi. He advanced the opinion that anyone would rather suffer humiliation than shield a criminal, and that if Hill had really been shot over a woman, she would have made it known before the trial.

The Supreme Court concluded that "the commission of the offense is beyond all doubt" and unanimously affirmed the judgment entered against Hill in May 1914. Not one of the judges had the slightest criticism of any part of the evidence or trial procedure. Yet anyone acquainted with the case must have concluded that there was a reasonable doubt that Joe Hill had committed the offense he was charged with. Men with considerable legal background, such as Ernest D. Condit, Wall Street law reporter, F. G. Derrickson, Manager, Legal Aid Department, M. J. Scanlon, Nevada state senator, and Samuel A. Carlson, mayor of Jamestown, New York, felt that there was a reasonable doubt and appealed for a new trial.[28]

On July 14, 1915, Joe Hill was removed from the County Jail to the State Penitentiary and, on August 2, re-sentenced by Judge Ritchie to be shot on October 1, 1915. Fear of an I.W.W. "demonstration" again caused the police to throw special protection around Hill as he was taken from and back to the jail.[29]

"What does the organization think proper action to take now," Joe Hill wrote to the Defense Committee. "My life is a drop in the bucket, but there is a principle involved in this case! And to be honest, I don't want to lie down as long as we have the least fighting chance."[30] But when it was suggested that the case be appealed to the U.S. Supreme Court, he was reluctant to sanction such a step, aware of the costs involved. "There has been enough of money expended on my case already," he wrote to Elizabeth Gurley Flynn on July 14.[31] At the same time, he informed Judge Hilton: "If circumstances are such that nothing can be done, I want to thank you for what you have already done for me. And you can just bet your bottom dollar that I will show this gang of highbinders, that are operating here in the name of justice, how a *Man* should die."[32]

Since an appeal to the Supreme Court was expensive and the Defense Committee was now entirely without funds, Hilton leaned towards appealing to the Board of Pardons of Utah for a commutation. He assured Hill that this held out little hope, "as the Board is composed of the members of the Supreme Court, the Atty Gen. and the Gov. of the State. These men have already passed on your case with the exception of the Gov." (Hilton underestimated the odds against Hill. Of the five members of the Board of Pardons, three, a majority, were members of the State Supreme Court who would be passing judgments on their own judgment.) Hill came to a quick decision—there was to be no further appeal. He instructed the Defense Committee "to not pay another cent to *anybody,* and that will, of course, close the case automatically." Money, he informed Haywood, could be used advantageously by the I.W.W., and "we can not afford to let the whole organization go bankrupt on account of one individual." In a similar vein, he wrote to Elizabeth Gurley Flynn: "We can not afford to drain the resources of the whole organization and weaken its fighting strength just on account of one individual. Common sense will tell you that Gurley."[33] To the people of Utah he announced that if they "want to shoot me without giving me half a chance to state my side of the case, then bring on your firing squad—I am ready for you. I have lived like an artist and I shall die like an artist."[34]

INTENSIFICATION OF DEFENSE CAMPAIGN

Joe Hill's decision to drop any further appeal was overruled. The I.W.W. vowed to "fight this to the very end." Elizabeth Gurley Flynn issued a leaflet which affirmed this decision:

"His [Hill's] exceptional courage makes his plight yet more pathetic and doubles our determination to save him. A few days ago he notified the Committee in charge of his case to drop all further efforts, as he believed the funds could be better used in labor's struggles. Of course, we refused to accept his noble sacrifice, but if we are to save his life, we must appeal to you for immediate financial assistance. Will you and your friends sign and mail the enclosed appeal to the Governor? . . .

"P.S. Word just received from Utah advises that Joe Hill is to be shot Oct. 1st, *unless we can secure quick action.* Will you help us?"[35]

Elizabeth Gurley Flynn's appeal, printed in leaflet form, was distributed by trade unions and Socialist Party locals. With Eugene V. Debs, among many, contributing his "mite" to the Defense Fund,[36] enough money was raised to continue the efforts to win a reversal of the death sentence. The decision, however, was not to carry the case to the U.S. Supreme Court on the ground that it would probably rule there was no federal question involved. Frank P. Walsh, chairman of the U.S. Commission on Industrial Relations, agreed. "You are right in excluding all hope of action by the United States Supreme Court," he wrote to Miss Flynn. "It never takes jurisdiction of criminal cases which have been passed upon by the respective states. In fact, through the interpretation of the various sections of the Constitution by the court, the right to a writ of error from it has become a mere paper one."[37] The Joe Hill case was then carried to the Utah Board of Pardons, which announced a special session on September 18 to consider the appeal.

Meanwhile, the defense campaign was not relaxed. On the contrary, the Defense Committee urged an avalanche of petitions to the Board of Pardons and Governor Spry. "The Time is Short. Act Immediately. Stop Right Now and Write down your indignation in your own words. . . . Hold Protest Meetings on the Streets and in

your halls. Raise collections, circulate subscription lists among your
friends and labor organizations At Once. Send All Funds to Hill
Defense Fund."[38] In mid-August, the awe-struck Salt Lake *Herald-
Republican* announced: "Governor Spry is being flooded with letters,
telegrams, cards and petitions against the execution of Joseph Hillstrom. . . . The communications come largely from laboring men,
Socialists, I.W.W. members and labor organizations throughout the
country." Petitions protesting the execution had been received, it reported, from 2,500 Scandinavians in Minneapolis; the Italian Socialist
Federation of Detroit; working men of Omaha; a mass meeting of
working men of Portland, Oregon; Local 192 I.W.W. of Balti-
more; Denver I.W.W.; working men and women of San Francisco;
granite workers of Barre, Vermont; Tonapah Miners' Union;
W.C.T.U. of Lode, California; United Russian Workers of Detroit;
Russian Red Cross Society of Chicago; "and many individuals in
various places throughout the country."[39]

One individual whose protest received widespread notice was
Paul Jones, Episcopal Bishop of Utah and vestryman of St. Mark's
Episcopal Church in Salt Lake City, the head of Judge Ritchie's
own church. Bishop Jones stressed that the conviction was based
"on purely circumstantial evidence"; that there was "no motive for
the crime" on Hill's part shown, and no previous connection shown
between him and the late J. G. Morrison. His appeal to the Board
of Pardons concluded: "The infliction of the death penalty on
Joseph Hillstrom may at some later date prove the State of Utah
to have been the murderer of this man rather than the administrator
of justice and thus mar the honor of our State and become a burden
upon the consciences of our administration of justice."[40]

Herman F. Titus, Socialist leader of Seattle, sent a letter of
protest to Governor Spry listing six reasons why he should commute
Joe Hill's sentence. The fifth reason read in part: "Joseph Hillstrom
is a man valuable to society and therefore his life should be spared.
He is no low browed villain. He is an intellectual man and a poet.
. . . It will be as much of a loss and disgrace to Utah to kill this
man as it would have been for Scotland to kill Robert Burns. Joe
Hill's song, 'Then We'll Sing one Song of the Poor and Ragged
Tramp,' rings as true to life as Bobbie Burns' 'A Man's a man for
that'."[41] On September 10, Seattle was the scene of a meeting at
the Labor Temple under the auspices of the A.F. of L. Central
Labor Council to demand "a new and fair trial for Joseph Hillstrom." The Seattle *Times* characterized the meeting as "remarkable

for its showing of solidarity in the ranks of Seattle's workers on basic principles of the general labor movement." A.F. of L., Socialist, and I.W.W. speakers addressed the audience. So decided was the unanimity of opinion regarding the case that the *Times* emphasized: despite the "widely divergent views on labor organization" held by speakers and members of the audience, "not a hint of discord crept in and by unanimous vote, resolutions were adopted protesting against the apparent injustice of Hillstrom's conviction and demanding immediate action by Utah's governor to stay action and give a new and fair hearing."[42]

Seattle was no exception. In many communities, A.F. of L. locals and individual members united with I.W.W. and Socialist Party groups to protest to the Utah authorities.[43]

The headlines in the Deseret *Evening News* in early September, announced that the battle for the life of Joe Hill had become international in scope. It disclosed the receipt of a letter by Governor Spry from Australia, dated July 13, 1915 (delayed because of the war in Europe and mail censorship*), reporting a mass meeting of "30,000 unionists" on July 12 in western Australia. Here "representatives of the working class and organized labor of Australia" had demanded "the instant release of our fellow worker Joe Hill. . . . Until this request is granted we have instituted a strict boycott of all American goods."[44]

By September 18, when the Board of Pardons met to hear pleas for Joe Hill, the flood of letters, telegrams and petitions pouring into Salt Lake City was such that an awed local reporter wrote: "No murder case ever tried in the courts of Utah has attracted wider interest than that of Hillstrom. . . . Considered in numbers it is doubtful if so many persons ever before expressed direct concern over the fate of a condemned man in the West."[45] One estimate placed the total number of letters as high as ten thousand.[46]

As the defense movement mounted, the authorities in Salt Lake City became panic-stricken and feverishly made ready as though for some gigantic armed invasion of the city. (Justification offered for these steps was that a few of the letters received by Salt Lake officials threatened drastic retributive action were Hill executed; actually, most of the letters were mild in tone.[47]) The police and sheriff forces were greatly increased. Pinkerton detectives were hired to guard the banks, Hotel Utah, Newhouse Hotel, and the

* The envelope bore the statement "passed by censor." (Deseret *Evening News*, Sept. 4, 1915.)

Mormon Temple grounds. The railroad yards were heavily guarded
to prevent the influx of Wobblies, and every night new arrivals were
driven out of the city. The homes of Spry, Leatherwood, Straup
and Frick were guarded day and night. There was even a rumor
that armed battalions of the I.W.W. would besiege the state prison
and attempt to free Hill. Accordingly, the prison guard was doubled
and machine guns, borrowed from the state militia, were put in
position at the prison entrance.

Hill was kept in solitary confinement, and no one was allowed to
visit him. Fourteen deputies armed with rifles surrounded the
hearing on September 18 when the Pardon Board assembled to
consider the advisability of commuting Hill's sentence.[48] It was
hardly an atmosphere conducive to a favorable hearing for the
defendant. For even though nothing out of the way happened,
though no evidence was produced that any plan to commit violence
was ever entertained by I.W.W. leaders or any other group, the
frame of mind in Salt Lake City was such as to make a rejection
of Hill's plea a foregone conclusion. The fourteen armed guards
standing outside the hearing building were a constant reminder
that the defendant was a member of the "dangerous element"
threatening the city. And a committee representing the I.W.W. and
invited by Joe Hill to sit in on the hearings was still another
reminder.[49]

THE PARDON BOARD

The major points in the defense case for commutation were:
(1) The evidence was insufficient to warrant conviction; the trial
was legal, but the outcome was unjust. (2) The Supreme Court
inferred guilt from Hill's refusal to testify. (3) The death penalty
is barbarous and should not be imposed by judicial decree, especially in a case based only on circumstantial evidence. (4) Convictions on circumstantial evidence frequently are proved erroneous,
sometimes after the innocent man's life has been taken; therefore,
Hill should not be executed. Time was needed for the truth to
emerge.

Judge Hilton cited the Pelican Point Case, Utah, 1896, where a
prosecution was based on circumstantial evidence and the defendant
was later found to be innocent. He pleaded that the Board had it
in its power to release Hill in the same way that the Governor of
Georgia had commuted Leo Frank's death sentence in the celebrated

case where, though nothing wrong could be found in the court record, it was obvious that a poor and weak defense had been the basis of the conviction. Hilton strongly asserted his belief in Hill's innocence and pleaded with the Board to recognize that circumstantial evidence in a homicidal case was always dangerous and should never be the basis for a conviction.[50]

There seems to have been some disagreement between Hill and his attorneys, for Hill refused to settle for a commutation, insisting that he must be granted a new trial. Following Hilton's appeal, Joe Hill arose and, according to the account in the Salt Lake *Tribune,* guaranteed the Board—in the case of a new trial—"to prove absolutely my innocence and to send four or five perjurors to the penitentiary where they belong." Asked why he had not brought forward this proof at his trial, he replied: "There was so much confusion at my trial, and my attorney didn't carry on my case properly. I didn't think it was necessary to prove my innocence. I always thought a man was presumed to be innocent until he was convicted. Anyhow, I never thought I was going to be convicted on such ridiculous evidence." The Board interrupted him to point out that it did not have the power to grant him a new trial. "You had the power to deny me a new trial," Hill shot back. "Why can't you grant me one now?"

But the Board was interested only in any new evidence that Joe Hill could present at the hearings that might tend to throw more light on his contention that he was innocent. In answer to the offer of a commutation on the basis of new evidence, Hill replied: "It is not commutation of sentence I want. It is a complete acquittal. With a new trial I can prove that I am innocent. My last trial was not fair. I don't want a pardon either. That is humiliating. I want an acquittal by a jury. I want to show up the things that are going on in the courtroom. If I cannot have a new trial I have nothing more to say."[51]

The Pardon Board unanimously rejected the defense attorneys' petition for commutation the day of the hearing, but did not explain the action until a week later when Straup submitted a lengthy statement to the Salt Lake City press. Acting as spokesman for the board, Straup insisted that after a man has been convicted, the burden is upon him to show why he should be granted clemency or have his sentence commuted; and this he could do only by submitting new evidence. What they really required, therefore, was that Hill completely exonerate himself by explaining his wound.

Indeed, they admitted as much: "So here, if the applicant claimed that the wound was produced in a quarrel over a woman, then it was his duty, and he was afforded full opportunity, to bring forward something to support it."[52]

In its haste to send Joe Hill to the firing squad, the Board even argued, in answering defense counsel's argument that past errors in circumstantial cases resulted often in killing the innocent, that the "conviction here does not rest on circumstantial evidence alone. *There is direct evidence, testimony of eye witnesses* to identify the applicant as one of the perpetrators of the crime."[53] This is an incredible statement. By what stretch of imagination could the "similar in general build and height" description furnished by Merlin be called direct evidence? Yet no one else saw any part of the murder. Certainly, no one in the slightest sense familiar with legal evidence could argue that the testimonies of Seeley, Mahan, and Hansen were direct evidence of guilt. The truth is that the Board wanted Hill executed and threw legal considerations out of the window to achieve this objective.

As Hilton noted in a statement to the Salt Lake *Telegram,* the Board's finding only underscored "the iniquitous system of having a Pardon Board constituted of five members, all but one of whom had already prejudged the case and solemnly announced that the accused was guilty. . . . What else could be expected than they should find against Hillstrom. It would have been marvelous had it been otherwise." Carefully weighing his words, he remarked that on the basis of his long legal experience, "I can say without the slightest hesitation that the trial which resulted in Hillstrom's conviction was the most unjust, wicked and farcical travesty on justice that has ever occurred in the West."[54]

The Salt Lake City newspapers praised the Board "in making the denial, disregarding threats contained in thousands of letters made by the I.W.W. and individuals from various parts of the country," and gleefully announced that Joe Hill had exhausted every means "to prevent his paying the death penalty."[55] The papers were somewhat premature. On September 20, the *Telegram* announced a new development in the case: appeals had been sent to the diplomatic representatives of the Swedish government in San Francisco and Washington asking them "to bring the case to the proper authorities and see that Hillstrom is not sent to his death without a 'fair trial.' " The appeals came from 25 women, headed by Caroline A. Whitney, appointed by the California suffrage association.

SWEDISH MINISTER EKENGREN APPEALS TO SPRY

This was only one of a number of such appeals received by W. A. F. Ekengren, Swedish Minister to the United States. Since Joe Hill was a Swedish citizen, the Defense Committee and others associated with the campaign had communicated directly with Minister Ekengren.[56] These included Virginia Snow Stephen, who had been instrumental in bringing Hilton into the case, Sigrid Bolin, sister of Professor Jakob Bolin of the University of Utah and former Swedish consul in Salt Lake City, Thowald Arnoldson, head of the department of modern languages at the University, and Oscar W. Larson, president of the Salt Lake City branch of the Verdandi, the most powerful Swedish organization in America. They also cabled the Burgomaster of Stockholm and various members of the Swedish Parliament asking them to appeal to the Minister in the United States. Swedish trade unionists of San Francisco cabled the Swedish Trade Union Council and the Swedish Central Labor Party, and many individual Swedes wrote or cabled the Swedish government to act in behalf of Hill.[57]

The Swedish government thereupon instructed its minister in the United States to investigate the situation of its citizen facing death.[58] In September Minister Ekengren wired Oscar W. Carlson, Swedish vice consul in Utah, instructing him to investigate the case, ascertain whether there were any grounds on which "stay of execution could be asked," and relay his opinion as to Hill's guilt and whether a "protest against the court's judgment" was warranted.[59] Carlson, who was later accused of having been influenced "by his business connections in that community [Salt Lake City],"[60] immediately wired back: "Have ascertained no substantial grounds on which to ask stay of execution. Defendant has been extended rights and privileges accorded him by the law. . . . All proceedings have been lawful and regular." There was, in short, no reason for "a protest against the court's judgment."[61] If Carlson believed this would end the matter so far as the Swedish minister was concerned, he was greatly mistaken.[62] Letters and telegrams poured into Ekengren's office, many in Swedish from Swedes and Swedish organizations in the United States, expressing belief in Hill's innocence and calling upon Ekengren to appeal to the Secretary of State to delay the execution.[63] On September 22, Jerome B. Sabath, Secretary of the National Association for the Abolition of Capital Punishment, sent Ekengren a lengthy memorandum based on its legal adviser's investigation of the case. After recounting the full story of the murders, the arrest of Hill, his trial and the appeal to the Supreme Court, the document concluded that "on strictly circumstantial evidence, of the very weakest kind imaginable, and without any actual identification, without proof of motive, and not beyond a reasonable doubt, a conviction of the defendant was had." Sabath assured Ekengren that the Association was convinced that if a stay of execution was granted, "the innocence of Hillstrom can be established," and, like the other correspondents, he urged the Minister to appeal to the Secretary of State.[64]

On September 24, Ekengren received a wire from Frank B. Scott, Hill's former counsel, sent at the request of the Eastern Swedish Club. Scott stated flatly that "Evidence failed absolutely to prove his [Hill's] guilt."[65] This convinced Ekengren to act; he wired Mrs. J. Sargent Cram, a liberal New York socialite, that "in consequence [of information from Scott] . . . I feel justified in applying through Department of State in Washington for a postponement of his execution. I am not at all certain of success."[66] He also informed Carlson in Salt Lake City: "I am asking for postponement of execution through Department of State," and instructed the vice consul to do what he could for Joe Hill and to confer with his attorneys.[67]

On September 25, Ekengren telegraphed Francis L. Polk, Acting Secretary of State, informing him that although he had had no opportunity to study the case, he was impressed by the "numerous applications . . . addressed to me to intercede in his [Hill's] behalf on the ground that evidence of his guilt is insufficient and that an execution of sentence would be a grave injustice." Hence he felt justified in asking whether, through State Department intervention, a postponement of the execution of the sentence "could not be obtained in order to have the case of the convicted further looked into." Polk forwarded this telegram to Governor Spry the same day, with the brief comment: "I shall be glad if you give this request of the Swedish Minister careful attention." He noted that this was done "simply as a matter of courtesy"; the State Department "has absolutely no jurisdiction in this case which is wholly in the hands of the Utah authorities," and that with the forwarding of Ekengren's telegram, "the case is closed as far as the State Department is concerned."[68]

On September 26 Governor Spry replied to Polk. The Swedish Minister's telegram had been considered at a special meeting of the

Board of Pardons, and it was unanimously decided that there was no justification for his request. Carlson, the local Swedish consul, had informed the Board (and communicated this to Minister Ekengren) that his study of the record convinced him that Hill had had a fair trial. Spry complained that "from unfair reports sent out by some of his [Hill's] counsel and by other partisans respecting his trial, many have been poorly misinformed as to the real facts of the case," but he was convinced that upon studying the record, which he enclosed, the State Department and Minister Ekengren would reach the conclusion "that Hillstrom had a fair trial" and was properly found guilty. However, he and other members of the Board of Pardons awaited "any further request you may deem proper."[69] The State Department forwarded Spry's telegram and the record of the case to Ekengren. Meanwhile, Spry let it be known that a reprieve would be given only at the direct request of the State Department, and since the State Department had said that it had "no jurisdiction," the Swedish government's efforts to stay the impending execution seemed to be getting nowhere.[70]

The State Department refused to intervene. To all letters and telegrams asking for such action,* Polk simply forwarded a copy of Governor Spry's communication asserting that Hill had had a fair trial and was properly found guilty. To Senator Lane of Oregon, Polk wired: "Department is not advised of facts of case and does not therefore feel warranted in taking further action in matter at present time."[71] All the State Department did when asked by Minister Ekengren for "a postponement of the execution of the accused . . . in order to institute further investigation of his guilt," was to transmit the request to Governor Spry without comment.[72]

MINISTER EKENGREN APPEALS AGAIN TO SPRY

Meanwhile, Ekengren was studying the Supreme Court's decision in the case,† and reading letters from all over the country. Among them was one from Jane Addams, head of Chicago's Hull House, endorsing the view of William L. Chenery of the Chicago *Herald*

---

* One telegram, dated Sept. 27, 1915, read: "Ten thousand Organized Painters Chicago Demand That You Get Stay of Execution for Joseph Hillstrom Sentenced to be Shot October 1st Salt Lake City. W. E. Germer, P.D.C. No. 14, Chicago." (State Department File 311.582355/original thru 35, National Archives.)

† Carlson had sent Ekengren a copy of State v. Hillstrom, 150 Pacific Reporter, p. 935 *et passim*.

which Miss Addams described as "one of the conservative papers of Chicago." Chenery, who wrote Ekengren at Haywood's suggestion, noted that he spoke up for Hill "upon the general ground that I doubt that any Industrial Worker could obtain an unprejudiced trial in Utah, and upon the further ground that I am opposed to capital punishment." In his letter to Miss Addams, Chenery put it this way:

"I wrote to Mr. Ekengren . . . on the general ground of my aversion to capital punishment and of my belief that no I.W.W. could get a fair hearing in so reactionary a state as Utah. I have just read the American Association of University Professors' Report on the conditions at the University of Utah. They are amazingly bad even for a bad year and certainly do not warrant the belief that justice could be dealt to poor radicals."[73]*

Chenery's view was also endorsed by Theodora Pollok of Oakland, California, who informed Ekengren that as a representative of a group of club women and social workers, she had recently visited Salt Lake City to investigate the case of Joe Hill. She became fully convinced that Hill was convicted solely on circumstantial evidence in a trial that "was irregular and prejudiced and [with] procedure unprecedented in criminal cases." She also discovered that "prejudice against Hillstrom's labor affiliation was so great that otherwise stern disbelievers in capital punishment refused to ask commutation and sympathetic professional men feared assisting me." In a follow-up letter, Miss Pollok noted that "the matter of real importance which developed from my trip to Salt Lake was, to my mind, the discovery of the feeling of the community in the case, a feeling directed not so much against Hillstrom as his organization, which made a fair trial of Hillstrom (in the human not merely technical sense) impossible in Salt Lake." All of the prominent people she spoke to reflected "the community feeling about Hillstrom's organization— their childish bugaboo, the I.W.W." One lawyer she met in a public hall told her, in whispers, that "innocent or guilty," Hill would have to die. When she asked him why, he replied, still whispering, "Because of the organization he is connected with." Then he added, "I'll be glad to give you any help and tips I can which won't endanger my own business interests." Miss Pollok then added:

* The reference is to the dismissal, and resignations in protest, of 22 members of the faculty of the University of Utah in 1914. (*See The Utah Survey,* April 1915, pp. 1–6.)

"It remains only to be said that Hillstrom's organization once struck on a job for the Utah Construction Company, which is practically a financial subsidiary—and a very powerful one—of the Mormon Church, and thereafter had to fight for freedom of speech on the streets of Salt Lake; and the 'Gentiles,' as the non-Mormons are called, are forced in Utah into a position of quiet subservience to the Mormon influence or into cooperation with the Mormons.

"Such then is the community from which Hillstrom's jury was chosen, to begin with, and which decreed the death of Hillstrom on October 1."[74]

On September 28, Ekengren sent an important message directly to Governor Spry, at the same time informing Polk that he had done so. It was a reply to Governor Spry's letter maintaining that the Board of Pardons could see no reason why a stay of execution should be granted since Hill had had a fair trial—as even the Swedish vice consul in Utah agreed. The Minister's message merits quotation in full, especially in view of Vernon H. Jensen's assertion that Ekengren "continued to press for a reprieve on the grounds that the case had stirred up unrest among laboring people throughout the world, rather than any claims of an unfair trial."[75]

"I have read the case of Hillstrom in the Pacific Reporter and must state as my opinion that while the procedure might have been perfectly regular the evidence on which the State bases its case seems too weak to warrant execution of capital punishment. The evidence is at best only circumstantial and though I know that there have been cases where convictions of capital crimes have been made on just such evidence, I consider it very grave to do it. As I understand it, it is a State's duty to prove beyond doubt the guilt of an accused. In this instance it looks as if the burden of proof were on the accused as if he must prove where he received his wound et cetera. His refusal to take the stand in his own behalf seems to have actually, while not expressly, operated against him with both court and jury. Further, even if it were proven that Hillstrom was one of the two men who entered the store it is not proven it seems to me, that it was he who did the shooting. He may have been in the store and yet neither fired a shot nor had any intent to do so. The other party may have fired all the shots. The question of motive leaves room for serious consideration, too. What motive could Hillstrom have had? It appears that he had been in Salt Lake City but a short time and could hardly have made such enemies that he would shoot and kill them out of pure malice.

From the information that I have on hand about the man I draw the conclusion that while he might be radical and haughty he has led a comparatively honest life previously and therefore, robbery as a motive for the crime would not seem much more reasonable than pure malice.

"To-day I have been telegraphically instructed by my Government to endeavor to secure a new investigation in the case and in their behalf and my own, I ask you again very earnestly to consider at least a postponement of the execution.

"I beg to assure you that I appreciate very fully that letters and appeals written by a lot of emotional people in various parts of the country cannot be rated very highly, nevertheless it seems to be a very serious thing to take a man's life if there is a shadow of doubt as to his guilt."[76]

APPEAL AGAIN REJECTED

Before he replied to Ekengren, Spry subpoenaed Stephen, Bolin, Larson and Arnoldson to appear before the Pardon Board to show cause for having brought "pressure to bear from the outside," an allusion to the fact that they had sent a cablegram to officials in Sweden. While Arnoldson said he had acted because he opposed capital punishment, Larson because he wanted Hill to live, innocent or not, and Miss Bolin because she believed he was innocent, Mrs. Stephen declared that she had done so because she believed the trial had been unfair. "I think," she said, "that the proceedings show prejudice—the prosecution often referred to the prisoner as belonging to 'that class who would rather kill than work'—and in other ways prejudiced the jury." She agreed with Hilton's opinion that "the trial which resulted in Hillstrom's conviction was the most awful, wicked, and farcical travesty on justice that has ever occurred in the west." Legal execution, she concluded, was the most cold-blooded, most deliberate form of murder.[77]

Having thus let it be known that he would not tolerate continued protests, Spry replied to Ekengren. He read the Swedish Minister a long lecture, bristling with hostility, in which he informed Ekengren "that the court and jury who heard the evidence and the supreme court who reviewed, and the board of pardons who considered the evidence in its entirety, are in a better position to judge of that than one unfamiliar with the record or the real facts in the case. . . . You have furnished us nothing except arguments from the briefs for Hillstrom's counsel." But the Governor himself had forwarded the records in the case on the basis of which Ekengren had drawn his conclusions! The moment these conclusions cast doubt on whether Hill had been guilty of murder and had had a fair trial, they no longer were adequate for basing a judgment!

In his letter to Ekengren, Spry aped the Supreme Court by contending that the case had not been decided on circumstantial evidence at all; there was direct evidence of Hill's guilt. He also made an interesting point to prove his contention that Hill was guilty. "Confessedly," he wrote, "two men with masks over their faces and guns in hand in the night time and for the purpose of murder or robbery, entered the deceased's store and deliberately shot him and his son to death."[78] There was certainly an important difference if they entered for murder or robbery. If for murder, then why would Hill have wanted to murder Morrison, whom he did not know? If for robbery, why deliberately shoot Morrison without even revealing it was a holdup? Moreover, Morrison and his son were not shot at the same time. The son was shot, according to Merlin's testimony, only after he had fired, or attempted to fire, at the masked men by reaching for his gun. All this pointed to murder out of revenge.

In his reply to Spry, Ekengren assured the Governor that he had gained his knowledge of the case "not only from Hillstrom's lawyers and friends but from the opinion rendered in the case by Utah's Supreme Court . . . and still fail to see that the evidence is anything but circumstantial." There had been no motive established by the state, and in view of the fact that the assailants had uttered the words to Morrison, just before opening fire on him, "We have got you now," it seemed to the Swedish Minister that it was "necessary for the State to establish beyond a reasonable doubt that Hillstrom not only knew Morrison but entertained malice for him." This the state had failed to do. The only thing it had proven was that Hill had a gunshot wound treated after the crime had been committed, "but I fail to see how it is proven that he received the wound in Morrison's store since not even the son of Morrison, who was in the store at the time of the murder, can positively identify him as one of the assailants." He concluded: "From my knowledge of American criminal law and procedure I form the opinion that Hillstrom need prove nothing until an actual case is established against him. Was such a case established if his identity was not beyond a reasonable doubt? It would seem not."[79]

In the flow of telegrams between Ekengren and Spry, the Governor had left the Swedish Minister one hope. On September 27, Spry wired: "If you know of anything or are able to direct us to anyone who possesses knowledge of any matter of fact or thing tending to justify commutation we will be pleased to consider question of further postponement."[80] With time rapidly running out, there was little Ekengren could do other than to urge Carlson in Salt Lake City to plead with Hill to provide some additional facts which could be presented to Spry. Carlson visited Hill twice, but the prisoner facing execution remained adamant. He was entitled to a new trial, and had nothing to add before that took place.[81] In desperation, Ekengren wired Hill directly on September 30, pleading for him to give some indication of where and how he had received his wound or at least to indicate where he had been that night. "I am doing all I can to head off the execution but without your cooperation I fear the results will not be good. Please wire me collect."[82]

No telegram came that day. Probably Ekengren did not really expect any, for he informed Spry that he had addressed Hill directly, "but I doubt that that will have any results since the man is evidently unusually stubborn and unreasonable." On the basis of his conviction that Hill had been found guilty on purely circumstantial evidence, and very inadequate evidence at that, Ekengren once again pleaded with Spry "to grant a postponement of Hillstrom's execution."[83]

This telegram went unanswered. "This is unfortunately all I can do in the matter," Ekengren replied to all who pleaded with him to do something—anything![84]

On the morning of September 30, twenty-four hours before he was to be shot, a death watch was placed over Joe Hill.[85] To Oscar W. Larson, who had asked Hill for "a biography," he wrote: "I haven't much to say about myself. I will only say that I have always tried to do what I could to advance Freedom's Banner a little closer toward its goal. Also, at one time I had the great honor of struggling on the battlefield under the Red Flag and I must admit that I am very proud of it."[86] To Ben H. Williams, editor of *Solidarity,* Hill wrote his "last, fond farewell to all true rebels":

" 'John Law' has given me his last and final order to get off the earth and stay off. He has told me lots of times before, but this time it seems as if he is meaning business. I have said many time and again that I was going to get a new trial or die trying. I have told it to my friends, it has been printed in the newspapers, and I don't see why I should 'eat my own crow' just because I happen to be up against a firing squad. I have stated my position plainly to everybody, and I won't budge an inch, because I know I am in the right. Tomorrow I expect to take a trip to the planet Mars, and if so, will immediately commence to organize the Mars canal workers into the I.W.W., and will sing the good old songs so loud that the learned star gazers on earth will once and for all get positive proofs that the planet Mars is really inhabited. In the meantime I hope you'll keep the ball a-rolling here. You are on the right track and you are bound to get there. I have nothing to say about myself, only that I have always tried to do what little I could to make this earth a little better for the great producing class; and I can pass off into the great unknown with the pleasure of knowing that I have never in my life, double crossed a man, woman or child."[87]

PRESIDENT WILSON BRINGS STAY OF EXECUTION

While preparations were being made in Salt Lake City for Hill's execution, dramatic scenes were taking place in Washington. Unable to get the State Department to intervene, the groups fighting for Joe Hill's life appealed to President Woodrow Wilson. On September 29, Mrs. J. Sargent Cram and Elizabeth Gurley Flynn appeared in the nation's capital, visited Joseph Tumulty, President Wilson's secretary, and pleaded for the President to ask for a stay of execution. Tumulty requested that Frank B. Scott, Hill's former attorney, wire him to appeal to the President and state his opinion as to Hill's innocence. Scott wired Tumulty: "Absolutely no evidence connecting Hillstrom with murder except unexplained bullet wound which he insists is no one's business. Three others with unexplained bullet wounds same night. Hillstrom fanatically makes no attempt to save his life."[88]

The same day Judge Hilton wired Tumulty: "Please say to President that Hillstrom's execution in Salt Lake City means judicial murder."[89] Tumulty then suggested that Ekengren send "a stronger and direct appeal immediately to the President," and Mrs. Cram, who conveyed this news to the Swedish Minister, expressed the sincere hope that "you will feel empowered to [do] this most important office for your unfortunate countryman."[90] Ekengren did not hesitate. He immediately appealed to Wilson, saying that he was convinced that Hill had not had a fair trial and had been unjustly sentenced to death:

"My opinion as to the injustice of the sentence considering the evidence produced at the trial is shared by several men of legal profession as well as by a great number of prominent citizens in different parts of the country and I have received numerous applications to try to intercede in behalf of the condemned. Also my Government which has from several sources received information about the case has instructed me to do my utmost."

Ekengren urged the President to obtain a stay of execution so as to permit time for the Minister to submit new evidence.[91]

President Wilson then telegraphed Governor Spry: "Respectfully ask if it would not be possible to postpone execution of Joseph Hillstrom, who, I understand, is a Swedish subject, until the Swedish Minister has had an opportunity to present his view of the case fully to your Excellency." Spry granted a reprieve until the next meeting of the Board of Pardons (October 16), but he insisted in his reply to Wilson that Hill was guilty and had had a "fair trial," and that he was acting "upon your request, and your request only." Spry sourly told the press "that it was the first time in the history of the country that he had heard of the President of the United States interfering in a state case."[92]

The death watch was removed. Reflecting on Joe Hill's reprieve, Charles Ashleigh wrote from Minneapolis to *Solidarity:* "Here . . . and everywhere among the workers was the triumphant sentiment, 'We have done it!' And so we have."[93] State Supreme Court Judge McCarty felt that this attitude was precisely why Governor Spry should not have yielded even to the request of the President: "the lawless element with which Hillstrom is associated, the Industrial Workers of the World, will construe the Governor's action as a tacit approval of their course and methods. I have no doubt but that hundreds of members of the lawless organization will swarm into this State and using Hillstrom as an excuse, create a reign of terror such as existed in the Coeur d'Alene country, at San Diego, at Seattle and at Goldfield, Nevada. If this course occurs only President Wilson is to be held responsible. . . . The situation is extremely serious, and apparently President Wilson has no faith in the Utah courts."[94]

The Hill Defense Committee did not relax with the announcement of the reprieve. "Keep up the agitation to free our fellow worker," Ed Rowan advised all Wobblies. Ben H. Fletcher, I.W.W.

Negro leader, outlined a nationwide petition campaign by which "250,000 workers and through them 750,000 others, will be aware of Hill's contemplated murder."[95] A tidal wave of protests inundated Utah officials, accelerated by Hill's courage while awaiting execution. A great protest on Hill's behalf took place at the Panama-Pacific National Exposition at San Francisco on October 2, 1915. Thousands of leaflets protesting Hill's execution were distributed near the Utah building.[96]

JOE HILL'S STATEMENT

From the day the reprieve was issued to the day the Board of Pardons met on October 16, Hill was subjected to a barrage of advice on how to conduct himself at the hearing. As we have seen, Minister Ekengren had already pleaded with him to give some indication about where and how he had received his wound, or, at least, to indicate where he was that night. Haywood wired Hill advising him to accept commutation if offered: "You will be worth more to the organization alive than dead. We will work for your vindication." To Ekengren, Hill replied by wire that he was about to release a statement fully explaining his position and why he demanded a new trial. "After you have read said statement I am certain you will understand me better." To Haywood he replied bluntly: "Will not ask favors. New trial or bust."[97]

Joe Hill's statement was published on October 4, 1915, under the title "A Few Reasons Why I Demand A New Trial." This rebuttal to the Pardon Board decision, written by Hill without advice from anyone, had been submitted to the Board on September 28, two days before Wilson had secured the reprieve. Warden Arthur Pratt read the report and then gave it to Governor Spry, who was to submit it to the public. But Spry did not fulfill the promise, and there is little doubt that, had Hill been executed on September 30, the letter would not have seen the light of day.[98] Since Hill quoted from the official record of the case, his statement is an important document.

Joe Hill presented a detailed review of the facts in the entire case. He firmly denied that he had killed Morrison, and said that he knew nothing about the slaying. He described himself as having worked all his life "as a mechanic and at times as a musician." He outlined how he had been denied a fair trial and why he had discharged his attorneys.* He declared his conviction that Morrison had been murdered by men who had known him and had entered the store with the express purpose of killing him, while he did not know Morrison. He refused to indicate where he was on the night of the murder or where he received his wound. "Where or why I got that wound is nobody's business but my own. I know that I was not shot in the Morrison's store and all that so-called evidence that is supposed to show that I was is fabrication pure and simple." Hill carefully analyzed why he could not have been the one supposedly shot in the grocery store:

"At the time when I was shot I was unarmed. I threw my hands up in the air just before the bullet struck me. That accounts for the fact that the bullet hole in my coat is four inches and a half below the bullet hole in my body. The prosecuting attorney endeavors to explain the fact by saying 'that the bandit would throw one hand up in surprise when Arling Morrison got hold of his father's pistol.' He also states that the bandit might have been leaning over the counter when he was shot. Very well. If the bandit 'threw up his hands in surprise,' as he said, that would of course raise the coat some, but it would not raise it four inches and one-half. 'Leaning over the counter' would not raise the coat at all. Justice McCarthy agrees with the prosecuting attorney and says that throwing his hands up would be just the very thing that the bandit would do if the boy Arling made an attempt to shoot him. Let me ask Mr. McCarthy a question. Suppose that you would some night discover that there was a burglar crawling around in your home, then suppose that you would get your gun and surprise that burglar right in the act. If the burglar should then reach for his gun, would you throw up your hands and let the burglar take a shot at you and then shoot the burglar afterward? Or would you shoot the burglar before he had a chance to reach for the gun? Think it over. It is not a question of law but one of human nature.

---

* Hill called McDougall an "honest man" who would have been of real service to him if "he had not got mixed up with that miserable shyster Mr. Scott." He was unfair to Scott. While the Salt Lake City lawyer was not very competent and may not have conducted an effective cross-examination of the state's witnesses, he always declared his belief in Hill's innocence and participated in the campaign to secure a new trial. However, Scott was criticized by E. D. McDougall for poor judgment in publicly replying to Hill, his former client, when he was seeking a new trial. This was in reference to Scott's letter justifying his cross-examination of Merlin Morrison. (Salt Lake *Telegram*, Aug. 25, 1915.)

I also wish Mr. McCarthy would try to find it possible to raise a coat on a person four and a half inches in the manner described by the prosecuting attorney."

Hill continued with an analysis of the bullet that had supposedly wounded him in the store:

"We will now go back to the bullet. After the bullet had penetrated the bandit, the prosecuting attorney says that it 'dropped to the floor' and then disappeared. It left no mark anywhere that an ordinary bullet would. It just disappeared, that's all. Now gentlemen, I don't know a thing about this bullet, but I will say this, that if I should sit down and write a novel, I certainly would have to think up something more realistic than that, otherwise I would never be able to sell it. The story of a bullet that first makes an upshoot of four inches and a half at an angle of 90 degrees, then cuts around another corner and penetrates a bandit and finally makes a drop like a spit ball and disappears forever, would not be very well received in the twentieth century. And just think of it that the greatest brains in Utah can sit and listen to such rot as that and then say that 'Hillstrom' got a fair and impartial trial."

Joe Hill closed his statement by appealing for support in his demand for a new trial:

"Now, anyone can readily understand that I am not in a position where I could afford to make any false statement. I have stated the facts as I know them in my own simple way. I think I shall be able to convince every fair-minded man and woman who reads these lines that I did not have a fair and impartial trial in spite of what learned jurists may have said to the contrary. Now if you don't like to see perjurors and dignified crooks go unpunished, if you don't like to see human life being sold like a commodity in the market, then give me a hand. I am going to stick to my principle no matter what may come. I am going to have a new trial or die trying. Yours for Fair Play, Joseph Hillstrom."[99]

NEW APPEAL TO WILSON REJECTED

While Hill's statement convinced Ekengren more than ever that his fellow-countryman was entitled to a new trial, he knew that nothing in it "will alter [the] situation."[100] He had planned to come to Salt Lake City and make a personal investigation prior to the meeting of the Board of Pardons, but, after consulting Judge Hilton, decided that such a step would achieve nothing "for gaining

a new trial." The minds of the authorities in Utah were closed, and
it would be "perfectly useless" to try to reopen the case.[101] As
Hilton pointed out, nothing would influence the Board "but new
evidence," and the likelihood of obtaining it in Salt Lake City did
not exist. "Hillstrom is quite resigned," Hilton added bitterly, "but
all the same, if he is shot it will be a judicial murder, nothing
less."[102]

At a two-day conference in Washington, Hilton and Ekengren
concluded that the only way left to save Hill from execution was to
try to obtain a commutation of sentence.[103] Hilton then drew up a
draft of a letter Ekengren should send to Wilson urging the
President to request the Board of Pardons to commute Hill's sentence to life imprisonment. It was a strongly-worded condemnation
of the trial and sentence which Hilton characterized as "a sad
commentary on the administration of justice in the State of Utah."
The appeal concluded with the assurance that following a commutation of the sentence, "his [Hill's] complete innocence of the
charge will be shown."

Ekengren toned down Hilton's draft. In a letter of October 13,
he pleaded with Wilson for action on the ground that since the
reprieve, his investigation of the case had made him "more firmly
of the opinion that the evidence and course of the trial do not
warrant the execution of a death sentence." Nevertheless, there
seemed to be only one way to prevent this: to secure a commutation.

"As the experience I have already had with the authorities of
Utah leads me to fear that representations made by me to the
Board of Pardons will be unavailing and wishing to do all that
possibly can be done I venture to once more address you, Mr.
President, directly in this matter. This time I would most respectfully ask whether you could consistently recommend to the Board
of Pardons of the State of Utah that the death sentence be
commuted."[104]

Haywood, who had learned of Ekengren's appeal from Hilton,
was overjoyed. "I assure you," he wrote the Swedish Minister from
Chicago, "that every member of this organization and the thousands
of friends of Joseph Hillstrom will most sincerely appreciate your
efforts in his behalf. The world is already wet with blood and there
is no reason why the great State of Utah should add to the stream
by shedding the blood of an innocent man. I am expecting every
hour to hear some good news through you from Judge Hilton."[105]

The hours passed without bringing any good news. Then on

October 16, the very day the Board of Pardons was to meet, Wilson's reply came. It was a politely-worded rejection of Ekengren's appeal:

"What I have learned of the Hillstrom case has given me a great deal of concern and I wish most unaffectedly that it had been possible for me to do more than I did but, as a matter of fact, my slight intervention in the matter to obtain a respite aroused resentment on the part of the authorities of Utah, I fear, and I feel that anything further I might have done would have been without effect. Of course you understand that the case is entirely beyond my official jurisdiction."[106]

FINAL APPEAL TO PARDON BOARD

On the day before and the morning of the meeting of the Board of Pardons, Salt Lake City newspapers featured lurid stories of Hill's "long record of crimes." Explaining that officials had at last uncovered Hill's criminal career, the Deseret *Evening News* presented it as a public service since the case would be "taken up by the Board of Pardons at 6 o'clock this afternoon." It then reported that Hill had shot a deputy sheriff at Layton, Utah, on May 4, 1911, in connection with an attempt to blow up a safe in the Layton Hardware Co.; that he had been arrested at San Pedro in a streetcar holdup; that he had been arrested and imprisoned in Butte; that he had participated in the I.W.W. invasion of Mexico; that he had "helped transport dynamite from San Francisco to Los Angeles and San Diego in connection with dynamite outrages," and was "thought to have been connected with the McNamaras."[107] Much of this information, already aired in the press on the eve of Hill's trial, had never been proven, and even the Layton affair was shown to be false when officials of that area failed to identify Hill as the man accused of the holdup after visiting him in prison.[108] But the Salt Lake City officials, who released the long list of crimes, and the press, that published it, had in mind only what they could do absolutely to guarantee that the Board of Pardons would once again deny Hill's appeal.

Fourteen armed guards surrounded the room in which the Board of Pardons met to consider the Joe Hill case for the last time. Hill refused to attend the session—he had already submitted his plea in his public statement—and Christensen, who appeared for him as counsel, explained: "He told me that he has nothing further

to say to the board and for that reason he is not before you."
Evidence of the long list of crimes of which he was supposed to be
guilty was submitted as "verified by a prisoner in the Utah state
prison, a former accomplice of Hillstrom." When Christensen
questioned Governor Spry regarding this so-called verification by a
criminal, the Governor replied: "We were told these things in
confidence and so I cannot discuss the subject." Judge Frick added
that while the facts of "Hillstrom's past crimes were infallible and
concrete," they would not be considered by the board in deciding
the present case. Minister Ekengren's statement was introduced. He
pointed out that, as a result of the postponement of the execution,
he had had "the opportunity to carefully study not only the opinion
of the supreme court but also the stenographic records of the proceedings before the lower court, together with other available
documents in the case, and . . . I have only been further confirmed
in my opinion that the evidence against the convicted man does not
warrant a capital punishment. . . . Considering the weakness of the
evidence which, at best, is only circumstantial, I venture herewith
not only on my own but on my government's behalf to address a
most earnest plea to you, Mr. Governor, and through you, to the
entire board of pardons, with a view to obtaining a commutation of
sentence for my unfortunate countryman, if for no other reason
at least for the sake of humanity and comity usually practiced between friendly nations."[109]

This moving appeal was ignored. At the end of the session, the
Board of Pardons terminated the reprieve granted by Governor Spry
and denied the application for commutation of sentence. On October
18, Joe Hill was again sentenced to be shot—this time on November
19. Surrounded by heavy guards, Hill attempted to address Judge
Ritchie, but was interrupted and rushed back to his cell in the state
prison.[110]

Frank E. Lindquist, Missouri attorney, a former Deputy Sheriff,
Justice of the Peace, Assistant Prosecuting Attorney and Assistant
State's Attorney, expressed the feelings of many lawyers who had
been studying the case when he wrote to Ekengren: "The Kansas
City Star brings me the sad news that the Board of Parole has refused to commute the death sentence. I am not at all surprised. I
firmly believe that Mr. Hillstrom, by reason of being a member of
the I.W.W., had about as fair a trial as Christ before Pilate and Leo
M. Frank before Judge Roan." Judge Hilton, who was in Denver,
issued a public challenge to the Board of Pardons for any member

of that body to discuss with him on any public platform "the reasons for denying clemency to Joseph Hillstrom," promising to prove that "they are not founded on either the law or facts in the case, but are intended to and do delude and deceive the public." He also wished to have the opportunity "to refute, as I feel I can, among other things, the false, wicked and cowardly aspersions on his character— that Hillstrom has heretofore committed any crime or that he has now, or ever has had any criminal record—now for the first time so bravely urged as sufficient justification for taking his life." Hilton sent a copy of his challenge to the Board to Ekengren, and added: "I do not expect any reply to it, but if I get one, I shall be delighted, as I can rout them on every contention. They cannot defend their action, and they know it."[111] He was correct. The Board ignored the challenge.

EKENGREN'S LAST EFFORTS

Although the legal battle for the life of Joe Hill seemed to be over, Ekengren did not stop trying to find some way either of re-opening the case or appealing it to the Supreme Court of the United States. For this, he informed the Swedish Royal Foreign Office, "an excellent lawyer with the absolute best reputation will be necessary," and this would require an expenditure of $1,500. The Foreign Minister cabled: "You are authorized to hire suitable defense lawyer 1,500 dollars Hillstrom case."[112]

Ekengren received many offers from attorneys in a number of cities indicating a willingness to enter the case, but he decided it would be best to use lawyers familiar with Utah law. He first approached the firm of Van Cott, Allison & Ritter of Salt Lake City, but was informed that if the firm took the case "it would be a mere waste of money . . . as every legal avenue is closed."[113] Although Hilton agreed with this opinion, regarding it as "a waste of time and money and energy to have any atto[rne]y to endeavor to set aside the conviction . . . for any technical irregularity or insufficiency of any kind."[114] Ekengren persisted. He finally engaged the Salt Lake City legal firm of Pierce, Critchlow and Barrette to undertake a study of the possibility of securing a reopening of the case. The firm agreed to undertake the assignment, although it made it clear that "we had no sympathy whatsoever, and indeed, are very strongly opposed to the organization with which we understand him [Hillstrom] to be affiliated."[115]

Nothing of any value emerged from this action. The idea of pleading that Joe Hill was insane was discarded after an interview with the prisoner which revealed him to be "not an unintelligent man" and certainly not one with "an unbalanced mind."[116] Actually, the Salt Lake City lawyers found only one ray of hope: Under the statutes of Utah, the testimony of Dr. McHugh should not have been introduced in the trial, and there was a bare possibility that application could be made to the Supreme Court of the state for a rehearing on that basis. "We have very little hope of its success," they cautioned. In the end, even this idea was abandoned when it was discovered that Hill's attorneys had known of the fact that Dr. McHugh's testimony was "incompetent," but had not objected on the theory that physician's "declaration of the accused that the wound was suffered 'in a woman scrape' would help."[117]

While Joe Hill was deeply touched by Ekengren's action in engaging new lawyers, he regarded it as a wasted effort. On November 12, he wired the Swedish Minister: "Judge Hilton is the best attorney in the world. Please dont expend any more money on others. The case is closed. Now my friends know I am innocent and I dont care what the rest think. Hearty thanks to you and the whole Swedish Nation for your noble support."[118]

The gloom in the inner circle working to save Hill's life lifted momentarily when Hilton received an unsigned letter late in October from Buffalo, New York. The writer, barely literate, claimed to have been at the Eselius home on January 10, 1914, and recalled that at

"10 o'clock P.M. . . . Joe Hillstrom remembered of having an appointment with a woman acquaintience in Murray thereupon Joe Hillstrom left the house alone and walked to the house of said acquaintience and upon arrival He came in contac with a man how was in a great state of excitement and before they recognized each other the other drew a gun and fired the fatal shot through Joes body and in the struggle that followed Joe Hillstrom rested the gun from the man Whereupon Joe remarked that it would be a suvenir in case He Joe lived through it, and from there he went to Dr. McHugh's office.

"This is all I can say at present."

Hilton quickly forwarded the letter to Ekengren along with the opinion that it "impressed me greatly" since it gave all "the facts of the quarrel over the woman, and how Joe was shot." The Swedish Minister shared Hilton's excitement, and jumped to the conclusion that the writer was probably Otto Applequist who had disappeared on the night of the murder. Obtaining a circular with a picture and description of Applequist from the police in Salt Lake City, Ekengren forwarded it to the chief of police in Buffalo, urging him to investigate and report his findings. "It is realized that the letter in question might be written by just some crank, it is thought that in view of the importance of finding Applequist it would be wise to write to you in the matter."[119]

Meanwhile, Hilton had written to Joe Hill, informed him of the letter from Buffalo which "gives me for the first time knowledge of the real facts in your case," and asked for permission to make its contents public "and so save you from your impending fate." He implored Hill to cooperate:

"Now Joe, if I have ever deserved the full confidence of a client, it is in your case. . . . These my last words to you express the hope that you may be guided in your decision by a realization of the awful responsibility that rests on all and that in this supreme moment I may hear from you and that I am at liberty to make the facts public if they are true."[120]

The letter was never released to the public. Neither did a response come from Buffalo. Hilton was now convinced that it was all over. The letter from Buffalo, he wrote the counsel for the National Association for the Abolition of Capital Punishment, had been "the only hope." For Hill's life could only be saved by proof that he had been shot in a quarrel. "In my opinion, without this showing, Hillstrom will be executed no matter how many petitions are filed. I know what the Mormon influence means."[121]

MASS APPEALS TO PRESIDENT WILSON

As Hilton was writing, the campaign of mass meetings, protests and petitions reached new heights. Letters, resolutions and petitions continued to be directed to Governor Spry. Hundreds signed a petition which requested the Governor to grant the condemned man a pardon for the following reasons:

"That the said Hillstrom was denied by the Judge of the said District Court of Salt Lake County that fair and impartial trial which is guaranteed to all citizens of the United States by the Constitution thereof, and the laws of the State of Utah, in that the said Court denied to him the privilege of being defended by counsel of his own selection, or of conducting his own defence, and that he has therefore been deprived of the benefit of counsel.

"Because the conviction of said Hillstrom was obtained upon flimsy and wholly insufficient evidence, the said trial being a mockery of justice and the verdict rendered therein due wholly to prejudice prevailing in said Salt Lake County against Hillstrom because of his activity in the labor movement."[122]

Letters, resolutions and petitions also continued to arrive in Ekengren's office, many from Swedish societies in the United States and Canada. The Minister was urged to plead once again with President Wilson to stave off the execution of a man "sentenced to be shot on circumstantial evidence alone."[123] But thousands of Americans did not depend only on the Swedish Minister's influence to persuade Wilson to intercede once again. The United Hebrew Trades of New York City, representing 250,000 Jewish workers, the Ladies' and Dressmakers' Union of New York City, I.W.W. locals—indeed scores of unions all over the country—appealed to the President directly.[124] The A.F. of L. Central Council of Seattle urged Wilson to stay the execution "in the spirit of truest patriotism."[125] The International Longshoremen's Association of the same city wrote that "Joe Hill's death without justification will light an unquenchable fire of revolt in the heart of every worker in this community,"[126] and a mass protest meeting in Seattle, again under the joint sponsorship of the A.F. of L., the Socialist Party, and the I.W.W., wired Wilson:

"We consider it an outrage that a few men like the members of the board of pardons, can set their prejudiced opinions against that of a multitude and allow a man like Joseph Hillstrom to be killed, when a grand jury of millions of people in all parts of the world believe he has not had a fair trial. They have not produced evidence enough to warrant the killing of a dog. If Joseph Hillstrom is killed, under the circumstances, along with him will die, in the hearts of millions of workers, what little respect remains for the capitalist system and their institutions. We pledge ourselves to do what we can to overthrow a system under which such infamy is possible. We hereby call upon you to prevent the execution."[127]

Hundreds of copies of a typewritten resolution from Swedish-speaking people throughout the United States were mailed to Wilson. It pronounced that Hill was "merely a victim of a conspiracy due to hatred and prejudice on account of his activity in the labor movement," demanded that his execution "be stayed, and that he be immediately liberated or granted a new trial," and went on:

"Resolved, That, should contrary to our expectations the sentence be carried out, we shall hold the whole American people responsible for such an outrage, and be it further

"Resolved, That in such a case American citizenship has no longer value to us, and that we foreswear the loyalty to American laws, government and institutions which has heretofore characterized our people. For where law and government ceases to be the instruments of justice and are used for the murder of the innocent, loyalty ceases to be a virtue."[128]

Individual letters asking Wilson to intervene once again came from Helen Keller, I. Baer Rheinhardt, counsel, and Jerome B. Sabath, Secretary, of the National Association for the Abolition of Capital Punishment, Robert G. Valentine, former Commissioner of Indian Affairs, and many others.[129] Perhaps the most moving document in the voluminous file in the State Department archives and the Woodrow Wilson Papers was the letter to the President, written in pencil, from Bernard Kyler of Goshen, California:

"I write to you to save Joe Hillstrom from execution in Salt Lake, Utah, for the reason that Hillstrom is the first and only true composer of working class songs and poetry. Hillstrom is the Bobby Burns of today, and if Joe is put to death, the working class will lose a genius, who can if he lives, alleviate a lot of mental anguish among my kind. Joe understands our troubles, because he had had to sleep in barns and haystacks, and those who have never had to live such life can never understand the troubles we have in the jungles. At present I am working on the State Highway and live in the roughest way. This camp has not enough tents, and I must sleep in, and around some haystacks. Men in your position of society do not understand, but Joe Hillstrom does, for he proves it in the songs he writes. I do not know Joe personally but have seen and studied many of his writings, and think he is the greatest educater for true and sensible society. Hoping Mr. President that you do not let them put Joe Hillstrom to death, I remain your's for a true and sensible society."[130]

All of the appeals to Wilson already cited came to the President on or before November 15. They were unable by that time to produce any results. (Neither did a visit on November 11 by Mrs. J. Sargent Cram and Elizabeth Gurley Flynn who appealed to Wilson to intervene. While the President listened attentively, he only

JOE HILLSTROM
Protest Meeting!
I. W. W. HALL, 208 2d Ave., So.

Before the Board of Pardons, he said: "I don't want a pardon, or a commutation, I want a new trial or nothing. If my life will help some other workingman to a fair trial, I am ready to give it. If by living my life I can aid others to the fairness denied me, I have not lived in vain."

¶ To the press he wrote: "I am going to have a new trial or die trying. I have lived like an Artist and I shall die like an Artist."—

JOSEPH HILLSTROM

JOSEPH HILLSTROM
I. W. W. ARTIST AND POET, who is Sentenced to be Shot Nov. 19th.

"One of the chief causes of social unrest is the denial of justice in the creation, adjudication and administration of the law."
—*Commission on Industrial Relations*

¶ "I say without the slightest hesitation that the trial which resulted in Hillstrom's conviction was the most unjust, wicked and farcial travesty on justice that has ever occured in the west. To an impartial Board of Pardons I can easily demonstrate such fact without any argument. Only time would be required to read the record over once."
JUDGE O. N. HILTON

Sunday, Nov. 14th [8:00 P M.]
Speakers Representing
The A. F. of L. Socialist Party and I. W. W.
will Address the Meeting

A leaflet announcing a meeting to protest the impending execution of Joe Hill, to be addressed by speakers representing the A.F. of L., Socialist Party and I·W.W. The city was probably Seattle.

90

"promised to consider the matter."[131]) Indeed, Wilson did not even reply to the wires and letters. On November 16, Helen Keller telegraphed the President: "I believe that Joseph Hillstrom has not had a fair trial and the sentence passed upon him is unjust. I appeal to you as official father of all the people to use your great power and influence to save one of the nation's helpless sons. The stay of execution will give time to investigate. New trial will give the man justice to which the laws of the land entitle him." The following day, Wilson replied: "I was very much touched by your telegram . . . and wish most sincerely it was in my power to do something, but unhappily there is nothing I can do. The matter lies beyond my jurisdiction and power. I have been deeply interested in the case but am balked at all opportunity."[132]

HYSTERIA IN SALT LAKE CITY

In Salt Lake City preparations were again made for the execution. Newspaper headlines predicted an I.W.W. invasion to assassinate Governor Spry and release Joe Hill from prison to be followed by widespread strikes. "Mining industries, manufacturing concerns and cafes and hotels are to be the first targets for the attacks," the Deseret *Evening News* quoted officials under the screaming headline: "Salt Lake As Strike Center. I.W.W.'s Will Give Particular Attention to this City During Winter."[133] The same paper announced that Captain H. F. Gerry, nationally known professional strikebreaker, had moved from the East and set up business in Salt Lake City. Gerry organized the Intermountain Protective Service with himself as secretary and general manager, and publicly pledged he would break any strikes begun in the city.[134]

Violence actually occurred in Salt Lake City during the first week of November, but it was directed against the I.W.W. and not sparked by that organization. Major H. P. Myton, of the city police force, shot and killed A. J. Horton, an I.W.W. member, who was making a speech on Second South Street. According to the testimony of five witnesses, Horton was unarmed. Myton's only defense was that Horton had hurled "insulting remarks" at him. Although the press failed to reveal what happened to the case, it was generally taken for granted that Myton was congratulated and not punished for his brutal act of murder! Horton was given an I.W.W. funeral, complete with the singing of revolutionary songs. The service, the Deseret *Evening News* raged, was "very different from the usual funeral service. The name of God was not mentioned and there was no suggestion of prayer."[135]

Salt Lake City now proceeded to dispose of the chief I.W.W. troublemaker. Heavily armed guards were posted around all official buildings and the State Prison. By November 14, the Salt Lake City papers announced that everything was under complete control, and nothing now stood in the way of Hill's execution. Further protests in the city against the execution were cut short by the simple device of denying the use of halls for such purposes. One such meeting at Unity Hall, sponsored by the Liberal Club and the Verlandt Swedish Temperance Society, was to have been addressed by Dr. Isaac Hourwich, a Socialist from New York City. It was cancelled when the hall withdrew permission for its use.[136]

WILSON'S SECOND APPEAL

Then, on November 15, at the 35th annual convention of the A.F. of L. in San Francisco, Tom Mooney, as secretary of the International Workers Defense League, received permission to present the case of Joe Hill to the assembled delegates.* After his talk, the matter was referred to the Committee on Ways and Means, with instructions to report on the following day. On November 16, the Committee on Ways and Means brought in a resolution which pointed out that "Joseph Hillstrom, a workingman of the State of Utah, and active in the cause of labor" had been sentenced to be shot; that "the grounds for this conviction and sentence appear to be utterly inadequate . . . . and that the rights of the said Joseph Hillstrom do not appear to have been sufficiently, or at all safe-guarded, but on the contrary seem to have been violated to such an extent that the said Joseph Hillstrom did not have a fair and im-partial trial." The resolution then, in the name of the Convention, urged the Governor of Utah "to exercise his prerogative of clemency in this case, and to stop the execution of the said Joseph Hillstrom, and that he be given a new and fair trial," and authorized President Gompers to communicate this stand to the Governor, the Board of

* Earlier in the campaign for Hill, Mooney wired Governor Spry from San Francisco in behalf of the International Workers' Defense League, of which he was secretary and treasurer, and 53 labor organizations to protest the "legal murder of Joe Hill" and the "dirty methods used at his trial." If Spry was not in favor of justice, Mooney warned, he could expect to be treated unjustly himself. (Cited in California, State of, *In the Matter of the Application Made on Behalf of Thomas J. Mooney for a Pardon,* p. 28.)

Pardons, the Swedish Ambassador, and the President of the United States. The report of the Committee on Ways and Means was adopted by *unanimous* vote, including the votes of the delegates from Utah.[137]

Gompers' telegram to Governor Spry and the Board of Pardons enclosed the resolution adopted by the convention, and added: "The sentiments, judgments and desires expressed in the above are earnestly shared by me, and I trust that clemency may be exercised in the interest of justice and humanity." Gompers, enclosing the resolution, also wired to President Wilson: "May I not prevail upon you to exercise your great influence to at least help in saving the life of Joseph Hillstrom, particularly when there is so much doubt concerning his case."[138] The very next day, November 17, Wilson informed Gompers that he had again telegraphed the Governor of Utah "urging justice and a thorough reconsideration of the case of Joseph Hillstrom." Wilson's message read: "With unaffected hesitation but with a very earnest conviction of the importance of the case I again urge upon your Excellency the justice and desirability of a thorough reconsideration of the case of Joseph Hillstrom."[139]

The news of Wilson's action spread joy through the ranks of those fighting to save Joe Hill. "Our efforts may yet prove effective," the secretary of the National Association for the Abolition of Capital Punishment wired Ekengren.[140]

WILSON'S APPEAL REJECTED

Governor Spry was in conference with Warden Arthur Pratt of the State Prison discussing the plans for Hill's execution when Wilson's telegram arrived. The Governor hastily went into conference with Supreme Court Justices Straup, Frick and McCarty. After the meeting, Governor Spry sent President Wilson a sharply worded telegram rejecting his appeal, saying in part:

"Your interference in the case may have elevated it to an undue importance, and the receipt of a thousand threatening letters demanding the release of Hillstrom, regardless of his guilt or innocence, may attach a peculiar importance to it, but the case is important in Utah only as establishing, after a fair and impartial trial, the guilt of one of the perpetrators of one of the most atrocious murders ever committed in the state. . . . As to your suggestion that justice requires further consideration of the case, I earnestly submit that the imputation contained, not only in your message to me, but also in your message to the president of the American Federation of Labor, that this convict has not had justice in the courts of this State, is not justified."[141]

Only one newspaper in the state of Utah supported Wilson's stand; the Ogden *Standard* observed: "The President sent a request. He did not command. He appealed in the name of justice. What is justice other than the exact weighing of right and wrong? Is it a crime for the President of the United States to make an appeal of that kind?"[142] But this voice of sanity was drowned out in the chorus of invective. The Salt Lake City press was unanimously furious at Wilson. The *Tribune* condemned Wilson for having "cast a cloud on Utah's fair name." "He stepped from the dignity of his high office," raged the *Herald-Republican,* "to pander to the class consciousness that takes no account of facts but only of prejudice. . . . Utah will not forget." The Deseret *Evening News* had been willing to forget and perhaps even to forgive the President's "unwarranted interference to save the brute's life." But its "indignation and resentment" were fully kindled when the news came of Wilson's telegram to Gompers. Wilson, in short, had acted because of "the adoption . . . of a resolution by the American Federation of Labor," and in order to assure himself of labor's vote in the 1916 national elections.

Supreme Court Justice W. M. McCarty went further: "President Wilson's conduct . . . will undoubtedly insure him not only the vote but the active support of practically every thug, yeggman and ex-convict in the land as well as those of that class who are now doing time in the different state and federal prisons but whose sentences will expire in time for them to exercise their franchises at the next general election, and there are many thousands of them."[143] This was the language applied to the President of the United States by one of the men in whose hands the life of Joe Hill rested. And all because Wilson had dared, in the name of "justice," to ask for reconsideration of the case!

"Governor Spry Refuses to Grant Delay," blared the headlines on the front page of the November 18, 1915 issue of the Deseret *Evening News.* A second headline read: "New Evidence Connects Prisoner With Crime." Beneath was the fantastic story that in different places on the suit of clothes owned by Hill—the coat sleeve and the trousers—the name "Morrison" was printed. The clothes were said to have been worn by Hill when he was arrested and had been with the police for over 18 months, and now, suddenly, they had discovered that the name of the murdered victim was printed on the garments. "New and additional evidence to connect Joseph Hillstrom more strongly than ever with the murder of J. G. Morrison," was the way the *News* characterized this ridiculous story. Hill gave it its proper characterization when, upon being questioned by the Deputy Warden, he remarked that "some fifteen cent detective had put it there."[144]

A third but smaller headline in the November 18 issue of the *News* read: "Hillstrom Says He Is Innocent." Hill told the reporter for the *News*: "I want a new trial and I can establish my innocence. I will not explain how I came by the wound, because that would be getting down on my knees and begging for my life and I am not that kind." The reporter added that Hill "smiled as he looked up from a letter he was writing."

JOE HILL'S LAST DAY

During his last day, Joe Hill met with reporters and with a delegation from the Defense Committee, and sent off letters and telegrams. He had a long interview with a reporter for the Salt Lake *Herald-Republican* who observed: "Hillstrom was self-possessed throughout the final talk with the world he knew he must leave within a few hours. . . . Except for displaying the naturally-to-be-expected signs of his confinement Hillstrom showed no physical signs of breakdown. There was an absolute lack of nervousness. His hands, protruding through the bars, were reposeful and did not indicate any lack of control. During the interview his eyes were clear, bright and intelligent in their expression, never wavering at the most direct question. His natural sense of humor did not leave him in this hard hour." The reporter's impression was of a man "mentally clear, self-assured," elevated high above the "pall of doom he knew he was approaching. There was nothing to indicate vindictiveness, braggadocio or penitence in the man's demeanor. He seemed obsessed with a spirit of confidence and optimism."

At the end of the interview, the reporter asked Hill: "What disposition are you going to make of your effects, your little trinkets, and personal belongings?" Hill replied that he had nothing to dispose of and had never believed in trinkets, keepsakes or jewelry. "But I have a will to make, and I'll scribble it. I'll send it to the world in care of Ed Rowan and my I.W.W. friends."

Hillstrom then sat down on the edge of his cot and inscribed the following valedictory to the world:

MY LAST WILL
My will is easy to decide,
For there is nothing to divide.
My kin don't need to fuss and moan—
"Moss does not cling to a rolling stone."
My body?—Oh!—if I could choose,
I would to ashes it reduce,
And let the merry breezes blow
My dust to where some flowers grow.
Perhaps some fading flower then
Would come to life and bloom again.
This is my last and final will.
Good luck to all of you.
                                    Joe Hill.[145]

To the delegation from the Defense Committee, headed by Ed Rowan, Hill said: "Tell the fellow workers for me to waste no time in mourning, but to organize our class and march to victory."[146] The same theme is contained in the first of two telegrams he sent to Bill Haywood in Chicago: "Goodbye Bill. I will die like a blue rebel. Don't waste any time in mourning. Organize." The other read: "It is only a hundred miles from here to Wyoming. Could you arrange to have my body hauled to the state line to be buried? I don't want to be found dead in Utah."[147] Finally, to Elizabeth Gurley Flynn, who he considered "more to me than a Fellow Worker," he wired: "Composed new song last week, with music, dedicated to the Dove of Peace. It's coming. And now Goodby, Gurley dear. I have lived like a rebel and I shall die like a rebel."[148]

CHAPTER FIVE

Execution and Funeral

On the morning of November 19, 1915, Joe Hill sat strapped in a chair before a firing squad. Five men armed with rifles stood ready to fire. Four had live bullets and one a blank.

"Aim," commanded the sheriff.

"Yes, aim!" cried Joe Hill. "Let her go. Fire!"

"Fire!" commanded the sheriff.

Four bullets pierced the target placed over Hill's heart. At 7:42 A.M., he was pronounced dead.[1]

Buried away in the Deseret *Evening News* of November 19, 1915, at the end of a long account of the execution, was a dispatch from Seattle which reported that during an I.W.W. parade on the night of November 18, William Busky, 22-year-old German-American had been overheard saying that he knew Hill was not guilty. Later he signed an affidavit that he was with Joe Hill continuously from 1 P.M. to 10 P.M. on the day of Morrison's murder and that Hill had had no wound when they had parted. The affidavit was telegraphed to Governor Spry, but he let the execution proceed. A few days later it was disclosed that Busky had told his story to the Salt Lake City police soon after Hill's arrest, and that he had been forced to leave Utah "shortly after the Hillstrom preliminary hearing and told to remain out of the state." Governor Spry's threat to try Busky was not carried out; nor was any attempt made to disprove his charge, which reflected so seriously on Utah justice.[2]

Joe Hill's body was first taken to a local funeral home in Salt Lake City where it was viewed by thousands of sympathizers, each of whom dropped a red rose on the casket. At the funeral services held in the tiny chapel—no hall could be hired, for the proprietors refused to rent their premises—and while "several thousands were packed outside," Ed Rowan said: "He goes to a higher tribunal to be judged. That higher tribunal is composed of the great working class of the whole world. They will answer and their answer will ring from pole to pole. Authorities of this state will have reason in the near future to remember that they took Joe Hill out at sunrise and shot him." Then he read Joe Hill's last will.[3]

At the request of Bill Haywood, the body was sent to Chicago. A death watch stayed with it day and night at the Florence Undertaking Chapel. The funeral services were held at the West Side Auditorium. Three thousand persons crowded into the building, while almost ten times that number, who could not get in, stood in the streets for blocks around.

"The funeral was unlike anything ever held in Chicago before," a reporter covering the funeral for the Deseret *Evening News* wrote. "The red flag floated unmolested at every turn. Draped around the plain pine coffin of the man who was legally shot by the Utah authorities. No creed or religion found a place at the services. There were no prayers and no hymns, but there was a mighty chorus of voices joining in songs written by Hillstrom. Throughout the funeral he was referred to as Joe Hill. On a banner above the coffin and on the programs containing the songs which were sung was this inscription: 'In Memoriam, Joe Hill. We never forget. Murdered by the authorities of the State of Utah, Nov. 19, 1915.' "[4]

"What kind of man is this," asked another reporter, "whose death is celebrated with songs of revolt and who has at his bier more mourners than any prince or potentate?" Joe Larkin answered this question in a brief, impassioned talk: "Joe Hill was shot to death because he was a member of the fighting section of the American working class, the I.W.W. . . . . Over the great heart of Joe Hill, now stilled in death, let us take up his burden, rededicate ourselves to the cause that knows no failure, and for which Joseph Hillstrom cheerfully gave his all, his valuable life. Though dead in flesh, he liveth amongst us."

Haywood read the text of his last message to Joe Hill: "Goodbye Joe, you will live long in the hearts of the working class. Your songs will be sung wherever the workers toil, urging them to organize!" Then he introduced Judge Hilton, who delivered the funeral oration. For two hours he spoke to the crowd, describing "the brutal murder of a martyr to the cause of revolution," and about the proceedings before the courts and the Pardon Board. "Hillstrom refused to satisfy the curiosity of the supreme court justices as to where he received his wound," Hilton said, "and he was condemned not for what he did but because he refused to gratify the curiosity of the officers as to the place and circumstances of his wound." In summation, he declared: "You can now see the particulars wherein the trial was unfair, and that some influence was brought to bear upon the Supreme Court to persuade it into an attitude of hostility toward

Hillstrom. I do not say that this was done by direct influence, other than the imponderable and undefined but always apparent and dominating fear of the Mormon Church, and that the views expressed by the Supreme Court are in consonance with the views of the Church."

After the ceremonies in the auditorium, the funeral procession marched a mile, through streets crowded with mourners to the train which carried the body to the cemetery to be cremated.[5]

On November 19, 1916, the first anniversary of Joe Hill's execution, at the same West Side Auditorium in Chicago, Bill Haywood presented envelopes containing the ashes to the delegates to the I.W.W. tenth convention and to fraternal delegates from other countries. "These delegates," the *Industrial Worker* noted, "will make the final distribution of these ashes with appropriate ceremonies when they return to their respective homes and countries. By this means, the last will of Joe Hill will be carried out. The breezes will carry this dust to where some flowers grow, and they, revived and nourished, will bloom all the fairer, and the world will be that much brighter."[6]

The small envelopes containing the ashes of Joe Hill were finally distributed in all 48 states of the United States, except Utah, and in every country in South America, in parts of Europe and Asia, in Australia, New Zealand, and South Africa.

CHAPTER SIX

Repercussions

Hilton's reference to the Mormon Church in the funeral oration was a milder version of what he had written to Minister Ekengren on the day Hill was executed. "I wish, now, that the Hillstrom incident has reached its tragic close, to ask you, in your report to your government, to bear in mind the vicious and vile influence that has made this infamous thing possible—The Mormon Church—and to the end that your countrymen may be fully advised of the dangers that threaten to all who listen and are persuaded to come to Utah, by reason of the lying stories and allurements that may be held out to the uninformed." In reply Ekengren assured Hilton that

"I entirely share your feelings with regard to the sad and unfortunate outcome of our endeavors to save Hillstrom from his tragic fate. It is to me hardly conceivable how the entire judicial administration of a big and important state, a member of this progressive Union, can show such cruel stubbornness and such disregard for the strong and widespread public opinion so manifestly expressed throughout the land as to in face of repeated applications even from the President himself refuse to exercise such clemency as in any other civilized country would have been only natural.

"I certainly now begin to understand what the mormonism and its evil influence over the people, unfortunate enough to be subject to its power, really means and although I know that the mormons and their ways and doctrines are fairly well known in Sweden I shall certainly not omit in my report to my Government over the Hillstrom case to further enlighten them on this subject."[1]

In his report to the Swedish government, Ekengren emphasized that Joe Hill was doomed to die because he "was a member of the widely spread radical workers' association 'Industrial Workers of the World,' and had aided the cause of this movement as a songwriter and composer." Mormonism, "the main ruler in the state of Utah," was determined to see Hill dead, for "his membership in the Industrial Workers of the World was hated by the leaders of the Mormon Church."[2]

REPRISALS

The Utah Copper Co. publicly commended Governor Spry for his firm treatment of the Joe Hill case. Spry assured the company and other employers that he would be even firmer with other members of the I.W.W. and with their sympathizers in the future:

"We did our duty with Joe Hillstrom, and we expect to do it with his lawless colleagues that have recently infested the city. . . . Life and property . . . is [sic] to be protected, and if our city police department does not rid us of the dangerous and lawless crowd now watching every chance to destroy either life or property here, I will put a force that will do it. . . . We are infested with a veritable horde of law breakers. This city is filled with them. We are going to do it at once."[3]

The I.W.W. was driven out of Salt Lake City, and many who had rallied to Joe Hill's support also felt the claws of reaction. Even before the execution, it was rumored that Mrs. Stephen would be dismissed from the faculty of the University of Utah because of her defense of Hill and because she had played the piano at the funeral of Horton, the Wobbly killed by a Salt Lake policeman. The president of the board of regents would not comment on the rumor, but when the I.W.W. threatened to organize a mass demonstration outside the University, the regents hired deputies and installed lights around the university buildings as protection against what they charged would be an attempt to destroy them. Since dismissal at this time would have been injudicious, it was dropped. But when the I.W.W. ranks had been decimated in Salt Lake City, and their voices of opposition could no longer be heard, Mrs. Stephen was discharged.[4]

As early as October 21, 1915, the Salt Lake *Herald-Republican* predicted that disbarment proceedings would be taken against Hilton. "Instead of upholding the law and the courts," it raged, "Lawyer Hilton appeals from both to outlawry and to the mob. . . . He has mocked at justice and railed at the ordinary processes of the courts until these find even among the most abandoned none so openly inimical as he. . . . Whatever steps or lack of them his fellows of the Colorado bar may choose to take, there should be no question concerning the attitude of the Utah courts if he appears here again. . . . Lawyer Hilton's voice ought never again be raised in a Utah court except as a defendant." After his oration at Hill's

funeral was reported in the Deseret *Evening News,* Hilton was
called before the Utah Bar Association. He was to be ousted from
further practice in Utah because, it was charged, he had violated the
lawyer's code in his attack on the state judicial organization. He
had defamed the court system, the Pardon Board and the Governor
by declaring falsely that they were under the influence of the
Mormon Church.[5]

"I cannot be disgraced or humiliated," Hilton wrote to Ekengren,
"by being disbarred from the practise of my profession in that
state . . . simply because I tried to be true to Hillstrom while in
life and death. I shall not resist it as it is already decided on, the
same as Hillstrom's death, but shall view it as a compliment."[6] He
changed his mind, however, for a few days later, Hilton wrote to
Ekengren asking for the records in the Hill case which he had left
with the Swedish Minister. "I need them badly in the fight I am
making with these Mormons."[7] Hilton argued in his defense that
he had not denounced the Governor and the members of the Pardon Board as individuals or as judicial organs, but that he had made
an inclusive criticism of the political policy of the state. No one paid
the slightest attention to this defense, and on July 1, 1916, Hilton
was barred from practicing in the courts of Utah.[8]

REACTION TO HILL'S EXECUTION

Editorial comment after Joe Hill's execution was widespread. A
number of papers shared the feeling expressed by the Fort Dodge
(Iowa) *Daily Chronicle* that "Hillstrom was the victim of judicial
murder."[9] This was particularly true in labor and radical circles.
The Detroit *Labor News,* an A.F. of L. weekly, denounced the
execution as the culmination of a conspiracy to murder a labor
leader. "The state had cried vengeance; the state got it. Utah's labor
haters had cried for blood; Utah's labor haters got it."[10] Jim Larkin
was more specific. He said bluntly: "Joe Hill was shot to death
because he was a member of . . . the Industrial Workers of the
World. . . . [It was] murder most foul."[11] Anarchist Emma Goldman bitterly declared that "the state of Utah has polluted itself with
the blood of Joe Hill."[12]

Ralph Chaplin expressed the feeling of all Wobblies in his poem
entitled "Joe Hill." The first four stanzas read:

> *High head and back unbending—*
> *rebel "true blue,"*
> *Into the night unending, why was it you?*

> *Heart that was quick with song, torn*
> *with their lead;*
> *Life that was young and strong,*
> *shattered and dead.*

> *Singer of manly songs, laughter and tears.*
> *Singer of Labor's wrongs, joys, hopes and*
> *fears.*

> *Though you were one of us, what could*
> *we do?*
> *Joe, there were none of us needed*
> *like you.*[13]

The New York Times, while accepting the Utah authorities' version that Hill was guilty, expressed the concern that his execution might "make Hillstrom dead more dangerous to social stability than when alive." It predicted that "there will grow up in the revolutionary group of which he was a prominent member a more or less sincere conviction that he died a hero as well as a martyr."[14] Even the Deseret *Evening News* expressed fear that, in time, Hill would be lifted out of his grave "for glorification."[15]

The prediction swiftly came true. On every anniversary of Joe Hill's death, working people in dozens of countries gathered to sing his songs and pay tribute to the man whose conduct during his long torment in prison, whose flaming sentiment, high hope for the cause of labor, and passion for the working class, and whose love of humanity and disregard of self had stirred people the world over. By the 1920's Joe Hill had become one of the great heroes in the tradition of the radical labor movement in the United States. In 1925 Alfred Hayes penned the words that were later to become even more famous when set to music by Earl Robinson:

> *I dreamed I saw Joe Hill last*
> *night.*
> *Alive as you and me;*
> *Says I, "But Joe, you're ten years*
> *dead."*
> *"I never died," says he.*

CHAPTER SEVEN

Conclusions

Writing in protest against the dismissal of members of the faculty of the University in 1914, Episcopal Bishop Paul Jones of Utah who, it will be recalled, appealed against the execution of Joe Hill, made a comment which is equally applicable to the case under discussion here. "As is well known, but seldom mentioned, politics, finance and organized religion form a powerful trinity in Utah which touches almost every question of public welfare."[1] This "powerful trinity" decreed that Joe Hill must die, and it adhered to its decision in the face of one of the most powerful protest movements in American history.

In establishing the frame-up of Joe Hill, it is not necessary to subscribe to the theory advanced by many writers, especially those associated with the I.W.W., that he was arrested and charged with the murder of J. G. Morrison at the behest of the Mormon Church, the Utah Construction Co. and the Utah Copper Co. in a plot to get rid of a militant union organizer. Ed Rowan, who worked unstintingly in Hill's behalf, was correct when he wrote for the Defense Committee: "We recognize the fact that Hill was not arrested in connection with labor troubles."

However, when the Salt Lake City police and the Utah authorities learned, after Hill's arrest, that he was active in the I.W.W., his constitutional rights went out of the window. The Mormon Church, itself a dominating force in many Utah banks and industries, was a bitter foe of trade unionism.[2] The powerful corporations in Utah, especially the Utah Construction Co. and the Utah Copper Co., were facing repeated attempts at organization of their workers. These anti-labor forces saw in the Joe Hill case an opportunity to deal a powerful blow to militant unionism, and their influence over Utah's political leaders was decisive. The police of Salt Lake City, under attack for a long record of unsolved murders, wanted a conviction fast, and they went ahead to get one, regardless of the lack of convincing evidence. They were aided and abetted by the local press which, like the police, treated Hill as guilty long before the trial verdict. No newspaper, moreover, was more biased in its treatment of the case and did more to create the picture of Joe Hill as a hardened criminal and an enemy of American society who should be exterminated, than the Deseret *Evening News,* the daily news-paper operated by the Mormon Church.

Certainly, the handling of the case by the authorities was marked from the outset by an over-zealous desire to convict the defendant. The investigation to establish that Hill was the "killer" was poor beyond belief. The "identification" of Hill at the preliminary hear-ing was so speculative that it should never have warranted his being brought to trial. At least three state's witnesses altered their testi-mony between the preliminary hearing and the trial. Someone, per-haps the state's attorney, arranged for this complete reversal of testimony between the preliminary hearing and the trial in order to make the facts fit Joe Hill. Yet none of those who saw the killers would swear that Hill was one of them. All the so-called identifica-tion was circumstantial, built by indirection, by alleged similarities.

The fact that the acrimonious argument following Hill's dismissal of his counsel took place in the jury's presence certainly prejudiced this body against the defendant. The judge should have called Hill up to the bench or to his chambers and dismissed the jury as soon as the defendant arose to dismiss his attorneys. The fact that the judge did not do this but instead allowed the jury to hear all that took place in the dispute between Hill and his attorneys, was ground to have a mistrial declared.* Hill's attorneys should have asked for a mistrial either at that point or at any time before the trial was over. It should at least have been in the record that defense counsel asked for a mistrial. It is difficult to see how the Supreme Court could deny that the judge's conduct warranted a mistrial.

So, too, the fact that the prosecution emphasized that Joe Hill did not take the stand in his own defense should have caused a mistrial. At the very least, the judge should have stopped the prosecutor immediately and pointed out that the Constitution of Utah con-tained the privilege against self-incrimination and that the pros-ecuting attorney was guilty of violating the Constitution.†

---

* I cannot, however, subscribe to the thesis advanced by the Friends of Joe Hill Committee (*Industrial Worker,* Nov. 13, 1948) and by others who have written on the case that the judge should have declared a mistrial the moment Hill indicated that he wanted to dismiss his attorneys. If this is justified, all a defendant would have to do to secure a mistrial would be to dismiss his counsel and demand the right to conduct his own defense.

† In a case in Utah in the 1930's (State vs. John Cox, 74 Utah 149), the prosecutor asked why the defendant did not take the stand. The judge im-

There certainly should have been a recess of the trial to permit
Hill to retain new counsel. But the judge insisted, over Hill's repeated objections, that the two attorneys remain in the case as *amici
curiae*. Hill did attempt, under great handicaps, to assist his own
defense, but because of the antagonism between himself and his
counsel, investigation essential to his defense was never carried out.
Thus, Joe Hill was denied the elementary right to counsel of his
own choice. One can understand what Hilton meant when he wrote
in a letter to Joe Hill, discussing the question of appealing the case
to the Supreme Court: "The irony of the whole miserable matter is
intensified when we know that it could all have been avoided if
you had even a decent defense in the court below."[3]

Judge Ritchie deliberately defied precedent, even in Utah itself, in
his instructions to the jury on the crucial question of the nature of
circumstantial evidence—thereby making conviction almost a foregone conclusion. Leatherwood's closing argument portrayed a
ghastly murder for which Hill was not even charged, and, playing
upon the popular hatred of the I.W.W., created in the minds of the
jury an image of the defendant as a dangerous enemy of American
society who should be removed. One wonders how, in the light of
all this, Vernon H. Jensen can conclude that "From a legal stand-
point it is clear that Hillstrom had a proper trial."[4]

The State Supreme Court pretended that Hill had been properly
identified by direct evidence, although the entire case against him
was in fact built on circumstantial evidence and distorted testimony.
And, though it accepted the principle that the defendant did not
have to testify in his own behalf, the court based its decision on
Hill's failure to testify on how he received his bullet wound. Behind
this, of course, was the clear evidence that the decision was really
based on Joe Hill's I.W.W. activity.

The Pardon Board which rejected Hill's appeal comprised the
three Supreme Court justices who had upheld the trial verdict, the
Governor, and the Attorney General, all bitterly opposed to the
I.W.W. and enraged by the widespread criticism of Utah's judicial

---

mediately halted the trial and delivered a sharp rebuke to the prosecutor,
reminding him that the State Constitution did not require a defendant to
testify and that his refusal to do so should not be held against him. The
defendant was found guilty, appealed to the Utah Supreme Court on the
ground that the prosecutor's action warranted a mistrial. The Supreme Court
agreed that the prosecutor's conduct should be condemned, but refused to
grant a new trial on the ground that the judge had rebuked the prosecutor.

practices. Rejection of the appeal was to be expected. It is obvious that the majority of the Board members would not evaluate their own work fairly.

The State of Utah demonstrated a desperate hurry to execute Hill, and it was only a tremendous outburst of protest that staved off the execution for 14 months. The authorities could easily have solved the problem of trial irregularities by granting Hill a new trial and, at the same time, satisfied a wide body of the public, including men with distinguished legal experience, that held Hill had not had a fair trial. Is it even questionable that had Joe Hill not been a militant member of the I.W.W., he would have been granted a new trial?

Why should Joe Hill have wanted to kill Morrison? No motive was established at any point in the case, and Hill protested his innocence from beginning to end. Certainly an intelligent man like Hill, if he had taken part in a murder and had used a red bandana handkerchief as a mask, would not have kept it in plain sight in his room. He went to Dr. McHugh, who knew him, and he remained in the Eselius home, without seeking safety in flight. Strange conduct, indeed, for a man who was pictured as an experienced, hardened criminal.

A positive case against Joe Hill was so lacking that the Board of Pardons offered him his freedom if he would satisfactorily explain his wound. This he refused to do. It is not difficult to be impatient with this attitude, and many of Joe Hill's supporters must have wished that, if unwilling to testify himself as to his whereabouts on the evening of the slaying, he would at least present someone who would corroborate his general statement that he was not in Morrison's grocery store.

But Joe Hill sincerely believed he was standing up for a sacred principle. "If my life will help some other working man to a fair trial," he announced on September 19, 1915, through his counsel, Soren Christensen, "I am ready to give it. If by giving my life I can aid others to the fairness denied me, I have not lived in vain."[5] What was the basic principle for which Hill was giving his life? It is that under the American system of justice a defendant need not prove he is innocent. It is the obligation of the prosecutor to prove the defendant guilty beyond a reasonable doubt. In short, the presumption of innocence is the sacred right of every man accused of committing a crime. The jury, the Supreme Court, and the Board of Pardons violated this right in the face of the failure of the prosecutor to prove Hill guilty beyond a reasonable doubt.

To sum up, there was proof neither that Hill was in the Morrison store nor that either killer was shot. Certainly, if Hill had been shot in the store, the police would have found the bullet, for the bullet which pierced Hill's body went clear through it. None of the so-called identification witnesses identified Hill as one of the killers. Merlin Morrison, the only one who witnessed the crime, did not identify Hill.

It is a basic principle of the law that a man should not be convicted of a crime on suspicion.* Joe Hill was arrested and convicted on suspicion. He had the misfortune of being shot on the same night that the Morrison murders were committed. This caused his arrest as a suspect, and, under ordinary circumstances, the lack of any concrete evidence would have been cause for his release. But when the police and the authorities discovered who Joe Hill was, they and all other anti-union (especially anti-I.W.W.) elements in Utah had an opportunity to "solve" a crime and get rid of a militant union agitator. There was no need to obtain real evidence to achieve this goal. Suspicion was enough to guarantee that Joe Hill would be convicted.

Although the case of Joe Hill did not begin as a labor case, it speedily became one and developed into one of the worst travesties of justice in American labor history.

"I die with a clear conscience, I die fighting, not like a coward," said Joe Hill as he was being led to his execution. "But mark my word, the day of my vindication is coming."[6]

That day is long overdue. It is time a statue of Joe Hill was erected in Salt Lake City. On it should be inscribed the words: "In Memoriam, Joe Hill. We never forget. Murdered by the authorities of the State of Utah, November 19, 1915."

* *See,* in this connection, Thompson vs. Louisville, 362 U.S. 199 (1960), in which the Supreme Court ruled, in a case involving a Negro, that to convict a man on insufficient evidence or suspicion is a denial of due process.

Reference Notes

ABBREVIATIONS

AMFA—Archives of the Royal Ministry of Foreign Affairs, Stockholm, Sweden.
LC—Labadie Collection, University of Michigan Library.
State Department File, *NA*—Department of State File 311.582H551/original thru 35, National Archives.
State v. Hillstrom, District Court—In the Third Judicial District Court of Utah in and for Salt Lake County, State of Utah, Plaintiff vs. Joseph Hillstrom, Defendent, No. 3532, Volume II, Transcript of the evidence introduced in behalf of the defendant.
WSC—Wallace Stegner Collection, Hoover Institution on War, Revolution, and Peace Library, Stanford University.
WWP—File 2573, "Joseph Hillstrom," Woodrow Wilson Papers, Library of Congress.

PREFACE

1. Wallace Stegner, *The Preacher and the Slave,* Boston, 1950; Barrie Stavis, *The Man Who Never Died: A Play About Joe Hill, With Notes on His Times,* New York, 1954.
Other accounts dealing with the career of Joe Hill in fiction, plays and poems are: (1) novels: Elias Tombenkin, *The Road,* New York, 1924; John Dos Passos, *Nineteen-Nineteen,* New York, 1931; Archie Binns, *The Timber Beast,* New York, 1948; Alexander Saxton, *The Great Midland,* New York, 1948; Margaret Graham, *Swing Shift,* New York, 1951; (2) plays: Upton Sinclair, *Singing Jailbirds,* Long Beach, Calif., 1924; Louis Lembert, *Shackles,* Duluth, n.d.; (3) poems: Kenneth Patchen, "Joe Hill Listens to the Praying," in *Proletarian Literature in the United States,* New York, 1935; Carl Sandburg, *The People, Yes,* New York, 1944; Kenneth Rexroth, *The Dragon and the Unicorn,* New York, 1958. For the treatment of Joe Hill in American folklore, *see* B. A. Botkin, *A Treasury of American Folklore,* New York, 1944, and John Greenway, *American Folk Songs of Protest,* Philadelphia, 1953.
2. Wallace Stegner, "I Dreamed I Saw Joe Hill Last Night," *Pacific Spectator,* Palo Alto, Calif., Jan. 1947; Wallace Stegner, "Joe Hill: The Wobblies' Troubadour," *New Republic,* Jan. 5, 1948, pp. 20–24, 38; Vernon H. Jensen, "The Legend of Joe Hill," *Industrial and Labor Relations Review,* vol. IV, April 1951, pp. 356–66.
Wallace Stegner's article, "Joe Hill: The Wobblies' Troubadour" (*New Republic,* Jan. 5, 1948), in which he expressed the opinion that Joe Hill "was probably guilty of the crime the state of Utah executed him for," brought an

immediate reply from the I.W.W. (*See* letter of Fred Thompson, ed., the
Industrial Worker, in *New Republic,* Feb. 9, 1948.) But it aroused nationwide
attention when, in April 1948, the Friends of Joe Hill Committee, organized
by the General Defense Committee of the I.W.W., picketed the offices of the
magazine and distributed handbills headed: "Joe Hill, Labor Martyr, Libeled
in New Republic." On Nov. 15, 1948, the *New Republic* published a con-
densed and paraphrased version of a long statement setting forth the reasons
for the I.W.W.'s belief in Joe Hill's innocence. The full statement appeared
in the *Industrial Worker* of Nov. 13, 1948.

Unnoticed by the Friends of Joe Hill Committee was a statement by Wallace
Stegner, published a year before, in which the Stanford University professor
wrote: "It might be possible, if one wished to do it, to whittle the figure
of Joe Hill down to the stature of a migrant yegg." ("I Dreamed I Saw
Joe Hill Last Night," *Pacific Spectator,* Jan. 1947, p. 65.) Copying Stegner,
John Greenway in his *American Folk-Songs of Protest* reports the "general
impression" that "Joe Hill was a crook [who was] probably guilty of the
murder for which he was convicted." He concludes that despite "the little
that is known about him [Joe Hill], nothing is more certain than the un-
worthiness of the honor lavished upon his memory." (*op. cit.,* pp. 188–97.)

CHAPTER I

1. John Takman, "Joe Hill's Sister: An Interview," *Masses & Mainstream,*
March 1956; Joe Hill to Katie Phar, 1915, Wallace Stegner Collection, Hoover
Institution on War, Revolution, and Peace Library, Stanford University. Here-
inafter cited as *WSC.*

2. For a history of the I.W.W., *see* Philip S. Foner, *The Industrial Workers
of the World, 1905-1917,* New York 1965, Vol. IV, *History of the Labor
Movement in the United States.* An earlier standard work is Paul F. Brissenden, *The I.W.W.: A Study of American Syndicalism,* New York, 1919.
A brief and often sketchy work is Fred Thompson, the official historian,
The I.W.W.: Its First Fifty Years, Chicago, 1955. For a collection of I.W.W.
songs, pamphlets, cartoons and other educational material, including a section
on Joe Hill, *see Rebel Voices: An I.W.W. Anthology,* edited, with introduc-
tions, by Joyce L. Kornbluh, Ann Arbor, Michigan, 1964.

3. *Solidarity,* Dec. 23, 1911; Jan. 13, 20, 1912; Dec. 19, 1914.

4. *The Songs of Joe Hill,* edited by Barrie Stavis and Frank Harmon, the
only published collection of the complete songs of the famed Wobbly songwriter, lists 23 songs by Joe Hill. In his *American Folk Songs of Protest,*
John Greenway expressed scorn for most of Joe Hill's songs with the exception of "Casey Jones" and "The Preacher and the Slave." He calls most of
the others "in a literary sense . . . contemptible," a conclusion reached by
few other students of folk songs of protest. (*op. cit.,* p. 197.)

5. Stavis, *op. cit.,* pp. 3–18; Ralph Chaplin, "Joe Hill, a Biography,"
Industrial Pioneer, Nov. 1923, pp. 23–25.

One gets a glimpse of how Joe Hill's songs grew out of actual conditions
in a letter he wrote to Sam Murray, a friend in California, who had asked
Hill to write a song, while he was in prison, which could be used by the
Wobblies to satirize the San Francisco Fair, held in the midst of widespread

unemployment. "No, I have not heard that song about 'Tipperary' but if you send it as you said you would I might try to dope something out about that present; and when I make a song I always try to picture things as they really are. Of course a little pepper and salt is allowed in order to bring out the facts more clearly." (Joe Hill to Sam Murray, Salt Lake City, Dec. 2, 1914, in "The Last Letters of Joe Hill," *Industrial Pioneer*, Dec. 1923, p. 53.)
    6. Marysville *Democrat*, Jan. 30, 1914; John D. Barry in San Francisco *Bulletin*, Feb. 5, 1914; both in "Scrapbooks of Clippings on the Wheatland Hop Field Riots, Wheatland, California, 1913–1915," University of California Library, Berkeley.
    When the hop pickers on the Durst Brothers ranch in Wheatland, Calif., led by the I.W.W., rebelled, on Aug. 3, 1913, against abominable wages and working conditions, a posse called in by the Dursts attempted to disperse the striking hop pickers and arrest their leaders, especially Richard Ford and Herman Suhr. In the riot that followed the sheriff's firing a shot in the air, two county officials and two striking hop pickers were killed. Richard Ford and Herman Suhr, I.W.W. leaders of the hop pickers, were tried for the murder of District Attorney Manwell; and though it was conceded that neither had fired the fatal shot, they were found guilty of having incited the gunfire by their agitation to organize the hop pickers and lead them in the strike, and were sentenced to life imprisonment.

CHAPTER II

    1. Lowell L. Blaisdell, *The Desert Revolution: Baja California 1911*, Madison, Wisc., 1962, p. 139.
    2. *Industrial Worker*, April 11, 1912.
    3. Vernon H. Jensen, *Heritage of Conflict: Labor Relations in the Non-Ferrous Metals Industry Up to 1930*, Ithaca, New York, 1950, pp. 263–70.
    4. Salt Lake *Tribune*, June 1, 29, 1913; Deseret *Evening News*, June 10, 11, 12, 25, 1913; *Industrial Worker*, July 10, 1913.
    5. *Industrial Worker*, July 7, 1945.
    6. Deseret *Evening News*, Aug. 13–20, 1913; *Solidarity*, Jan. 3, 1914.
    7. Howard Baker to Wallace Stegner, Seattle, Wash., July 10, 1947, quoting statement of "Fellow Worker Murphy," *WSC*.
    8. Letter of Joe Hill in Salt Lake *Telegram*, Aug. 22, 1915.
    9. Ralph Chaplin, *op. cit.*, p. 212.
    10. Jensen, "The Legend of Joe Hill," *op. cit.*, p. 357.
    11. Salt Lake *Tribune*, Jan. 11, 1914; Salt Lake *Herald-Republican*, Jan. 11, 1914; Deseret *Evening News*, Jan. 12, 1914.
    12. Deseret *Evening News*, Jan. 12, 1914.
    13. *Ibid.*; Salt Lake *Tribune*, Jan. 11, 12, 1914.
    14. Salt Lake *Tribune*, Jan. 11, 1914; Deseret *Evening News*, Jan. 12, 1914.
    15. Salt Lake *Tribune*, Jan. 11–13, 1914; Deseret *Evening News*, Jan. 12–13, 1914.
    16. Deseret *Evening News*, Jan. 14–15, 1914.
    17. State v. Hillstrom, 150, Pacific Reporter, 935.
    18. Deseret *Evening News*. Oct. 4, 1915.
    19. "In the Third Judicial District Court of Utah in and for Salt Lake

County, State of Utah, Plaintiff vs. Joseph Hillstrom, Defendant, No. 3532, Volume II, Transcript of the evidence introduced in behalf of the defendant," 453–57, original in office of Clerk, Third District Court, Salt Lake County, microfilm copy in *WSC*. Hereinafter referred to as State v. Hillstrom, District Court. *See also* Deseret *Evening News,* Jan. 14, 1914.

20. Deseret *Evening News,* Jan. 15, 1914; Salt Lake *Tribune,* Jan. 16, 1914.
21. Deseret *Evening News,* Jan. 22, 1914.
22. *Ibid.,* Oct. 4, 1915.
23. *Ibid.,* and issue of Jan. 29, 1914.
24. *Ibid.,* Jan. 22, 1914.
25. *Ibid.,* Oct. 4, 1915.
26. Joe Hill to Katie Phar, May 7 (1914), *WSC.*
27. Deseret *Evening News,* Jan. 14, 1914.
28. *Ibid.,* Jan. 22, 1914.
29. *Ibid.,* Jan. 28, 1914.
30 Letter of Joe Hill in Salt Lake *Telegram,* Aug. 22, 1915.
31. *Solidarity,* April 18, 1914.
32. *Ibid.,* May 23, 1914; *Voice of the People,* May 21, 1914. Emphasis in original, *P.S.F.*
33. Zapata Modesta, " 'Die Like a Rebel': The Life and Death of Joe Hill," unpublished manuscript, p. 20.
34. Deseret *Evening News,* March 10, 11, 1914.
35. *Regeneracion,* May 26, 1914, in Joe Hill File Box, Labadie Collection, University of Michigan Library. Hereinafter cited as *LC.*
36. Deseret *Evening News,* Jan. 12, 1914.

CHAPTER III

1. Deseret *Evening News,* June 17, 1914.
2. Salt Lake *Herald-Republican,* June 18, 1914. My emphasis, *P.S.F.*
3. Salt Lake *Tribune,* June 18, 1914.
4. *Ibid.,* June 16, 1914.
5. Deseret *Evening News,* June 18, 1914.
6. Salt Lake *Tribune,* June 19, 1914.
7. Salt Lake *Herald-Republican,* June 19, 1914.
8. Salt Lake *Tribune,* June 19, 1914.
9. Deseret *Evening News,* June 18, 1914. My emphasis, *P.S.F.*
10. State v. Hillstrom, 46 Utah, 349–50, 373; State v. Hillstrom, District Court, 559; Deseret *Evening News,* Oct. 4, 1915.
11. State v. Hillstrom, 46 Utah, 350; Deseret *Evening News,* June 19, 1914.
12. James O. Morris, "The Case of Joe Hill," unpublished manuscript, 1950, *LC,* p. 26.
13. Deseret *Evening News,* June 20, 1914; Salt Lake *Tribune,* June 21, 1914; State v. Hillstrom, 46 Utah, 374.
14. State v. Hillstrom, 46 Utah, 374.
15. Deseret *Evening News,* June 20, 1914; Salt Lake *Tribune,* June 21, 1914.
16. Deseret *Evening News,* June 18, 1914. My emphasis, *P.S.F.*
17. *Ibid.,* June 19, 1914; Salt Lake *Tribune,* June 20, 1914.

18. State v. Hillstrom, 46 Utah, 347; Deseret *Evening News,* June 22, 1914.
19. Deseret *Evening News,* Jan. 15, 1914.
20. *Ibid.,* June 22, 1914; Salt Lake *Tribune,* June 23, 1914. Dr. McHugh's testimony at the trial throws considerable doubt on the veracity of claims he made to Vernon H. Jensen in 1946 and 1948 that Joe Hill had confessed to him that he had killed both J. H. Morrison and Arling Morrison. Jensen quoted Dr. McHugh as stating that when he saw Hill the second time at the Eselius home, Hill told him "as nearly as Dr. McHugh could remember: 'I'm not such a bad fellow as you think. I shot in self-defense. The older man reached for his gun and I shot him and the younger boy grabbed the gun and shot me and I shot him to save my own life.'" He also added, "'I wanted some money to get out of town.'" (*op. cit.,* p. 358.)
Jensen does not explain why Dr. McHugh failed to give this information to the police, especially since he was of such assistance to them in making sure that Hill was under a sedative during his arrest. As for his failure to mention this supposed confession during the trial, Jensen writes: "As a Socialist and a disbeliever in capital punishment, he did not want to see Hillstrom hanged. Considering the information given by Hillstrom as confidential and privileged and not wishing to harm him, Dr. McHugh divulged only the information directly requested of him" (*ibid.,* p. 360). For a man who "did not want to see Hillstrom hanged," Dr. McHugh volunteered new information about the size of the bullet that had entered Hill's body, which was only a guess and yet could be crucial in convicting him. Indeed, the whole tone of Dr. McHugh's testimony indicates he was doing his best to convict Hill. Jensen, moreover, says nothing about the fact that Dr. McHugh made repeated efforts, though in vain, to obtain the $500 reward offered by Governor Spry for the arrest and conviction of the slayers of Morrison and his son. It is clear that Dr. McHugh was strongly motivated by the reward in turning Hill over to the police, and had any such "confession" been made to him at the time, he would have reported it to the police. None of the newspapermen who reported in detail on Hill's conduct in the courtroom indicated that he was at all nervous or anxious when Dr. McHugh testified, as he would have been likely had he been worried about his "confession" being revealed. It is ridiculous to think that an experienced I.W.W. member like Joe Hill would have to resort to robbery "to get out of town." Joe Hill was accustomed to travelling about from town to town on freight-cars and seeking food and shelter in I.W.W. halls and jungles when he was not working. Finally, it was Dr. McHugh who actually turned Hill over to the police, and it was he who told them that Hill might have some connection with the murders. Having gone so far, is it logical that he would not have told the police that Hill had confessed to the slayings, had this actually occurred?
I have made efforts to obtain copies of letters said to have been written by Dr. McHugh to the Utah authorities claiming the reward, but my request to the Keeper of Official records in Salt Lake City has gone unanswered. Barrie Stavis informs me that he has seen such letters (Interview with Barrie Stavis, Oct. 14, 1963).
21. Salt Lake *Tribune,* June 20, 1914.
22. Deseret *Evening News,* June 18, 1914; Salt Lake *Tribune,* June 19, 1914.

23. Deseret *Evening News,* June 18, 1914.

24. Letter of Joe Hill in Salt Lake *Telegram,* Aug. 22, 1915.

25. *Ibid.,* Aug. 24, 1915; Salt Lake *Tribune,* June 20, 21, 1914. E. D. Mc-Dougall criticized Scott for poor judgment in publicly replying to his former client at a time when Hill was seeking a new trial (Salt Lake *Telegram,* Aug. 25, 1915). But McDougall was himself guilty of poor judgment when, in his closing remarks to the jury, he said that the reason Joe Hill had "made a stir in the court" and discharged his attorneys was because he [McDougall] had tried to get him to tell how he was shot. "He would have gone to the gallows without a murmur to spite his attorneys. He is that kind of man" (Deseret *Evening News,* June 26, 1914). Apart from the fact that such a statement was hardly conducive to inspiring sympathy for his client, McDougall knew that the "stir in the court" came a few days before the question arose of Hill's testifying about how he was shot, and that it revolved about the nature of the cross-examination and the use of the preliminary hearings.

26. Salt Lake *Tribune,* June 20, 1914.

27. *Ibid.,* June 20, 21, 1914.

28. *Ibid.,* June 23, 1914.

29. Deseret *Evening News,* June 23, 1914.

30. State v. Joseph Hillstrom, District Court, 449–50.

31. *Ibid.,* 484–87, 556–57, 609–11.

32. *Ibid.,* 454–55, 458, 484–85, 609.

33. *Ibid.,* 529–34.

34. *Ibid.,* 487–517, 559–98.

35. *Ibid.,* 455–58, 526.

36. *Ibid.,* 522–23.

37. *Ibid.,* 452–53. Whether both men were masked was never made clear. Patrolman Vance found a red bandana handkerchief in an alley near the Morrison store. On Jan. 12, 1914, the Deseret *Evening News* reported: "The red handkerchief [found by Vance] tallies with the somewhat mixed description of the Morrison boy, who said that one of the men wore a red mask. The handkerchief was identified by Merlin Morrison." On Jan. 14, it stated that Mrs. Seeley told the police that "one of the pair" she saw had a red handkerchief around his neck. Two weeks later, she testified that both men wore large red handkerchiefs. Obviously, after a red bandana handkerchief was found in Hill's room, it was necessary to have both men masked with such handkerchiefs.

38. Deseret *Evening News,* Jan. 14, 1914.

39. Salt Lake *Tribune,* Jan. 16, 1914; Stavis, *op. cit.,* p. 31.

40. Salt Lake *Tribune,* June 7, 1914.

41. Deseret *Evening News,* Oct. 4, 1915.

42. Quoted in Modesto, *op. cit.,* pp. 36–37. James O. Morris implies that Hill simply was unable to prove his point (*op. cit.,* p. 20). But would Joe Hill have gone to the trouble of visiting the store where he had bought his gun to search the records if he had any doubt that he was telling the truth? He had no way of knowing that the records did not include the name and caliber of the gun he had bought. Suppose if, as Morris implies, the gun was of the same caliber as the one that was used to kill Morrison and his son and the records would show this? The question answers itself.

43. Salt Lake *Tribune*, June 7, 1914. The Deseret *Evening News* reported on June 25, 1914, that "Attorneys F. B. Scott and E. D. McDougall are understood to have advised the defendant to tell his story to the jury. Attorney Soren X. Christensen advised against it." There is no way of checking the accuracy of this report.

44. Deseret *Evening News*, June 26, 1914. The closing arguments of the opposing attorneys were not recorded by the court stenographer, as prescribed by Utah law, and must be pieced together from reports in the press.

45. Deseret *Evening News*, June 26, 1914.

46. Salt Lake *Tribune*, June 20, 1914.

47. *Ibid.*, June 25, 26, 1914; Deseret *Evening News*, June 25, 27, 1914; Salt Lake *Herald-Republican*, June 26, 1914. All emphasis mine, *P.S.F.*

48. Brissenden, *op. cit.*, pp. 8–9. Emphasis in the original, *P.S.F.*

49. State v. Hillstrom, District Court, 627.

50. *Compiled Laws of the State of Utah, 1907*, paragraph 5015.

51. An appellate court can not consider remarks of counsel objected to and not properly in the record (State v. Haworth, 25 Utah 398, 68 P. 155, 1902). Ironically, Judge Ritchie promised Hill's attorneys that an appropriate record would henceforth be kept (State v. Hillstrom, District Court, 627–28).

52. "The prosecuting attorney should not appeal to passion and prejudice" (Carter v. State, 75 Tex. Cr.R. 110, 170, S.W. 739, 1914).

53. Abusive language is not permissible under any circumstances (Bishop v. State, 72 Tex. Cr. R. I, 160 S.W. 705, 1913). Calling the accused a hyena and a brute held improper (Callihan v. State, 67 Tex. Cr. R 658, 150 S.W. 617, 1912). Mere abuse is not proper argument (State v. Mircovich, 35 Nev., 485 130 P. 765, 1913). Referring to the defendant as a crook and perjuror considered reversible error (State v. Schneiders, 259 Mo. 319, 168 S.W. 604, 1914). Calling the defendant a miserable wretch is improper (People v. Rotx, 261 Ill. 239, 103 N.W. 1007, 1914). Using epithets in reference to the accused is improper (State v. Pasco, 239 Mo. 535, 114, S.W. 449, 1912). Comments on the defendant's character are prejudicial error (Fish v. United States, 215 F. 544, 132 C.C.A., 56, L.R.A., 1915).

Leatherwood was also in error in attacking attorney McDougall. ("It is improper for attorneys to make remarks reflecting on opposing counsel." Roge v. State, 80 Okla. Cr. 226, 127 P 365, 1912.)

54. Clinton v. State, 53 Fla. 98, 34 So. 312, 1907. *See also* Morris, *op. cit.*, p. 42.

55. State v. Hillstrom, District Court, 619–24: Salt Lake *Tribune*, June 27, 1914.

56. State v. Hillstrom, District Court, 619–26.

57. Morris, *op. cit.*, p. 46.

58. People v. Scott, 10 Utah 217, 37 P. 335, 1894; State v. Hayes, 14 Utah 118, 46 P. 752, 1896; State v. McKee, 17 Utah 370, 53 P. 733, 1898.

59. Salt Lake *Tribune*, June 27, 1914.

60. Deseret *Evening News*, June 27, 1914.

61. *Ibid.*

62. Salt Lake *Tribune*, June 28, 1914.

63. *Ibid.*, June 21, 1914. A *Tribune* reporter interviewed Hill in jail and reported him as saying: "There are some defects in the harmony of my compositions, but that is because of my lack of technical training. I am a man

THE CASE OF JOE HILL

of little education and my modest accomplishments are due to a natural taste and some native talent in that direction. I have written lots of verses and songs and composed the music for some of them. Most of the poems are of a revolutionary character and have been adopted by the revolutionary forces, such as the I.W.W. and the Socialist organizations." (Salt Lake *Tribune,* June 21, 1914.)

64. Deseret *Evening News,* June 27, 1914.
65. *Ibid.,* July 8, 1914; Salt Lake *Tribune,* July 9, 1914.

CHAPTER IV

1. Ed Rowan in *Solidarity,* May 23, 1914 and Geo. Childs in *ibid.,* Sept. 26, 1914.
2. *Solidarity,* May 23, 1914.
3. *Ibid.,* July 11, 1914.
4. Deseret *Evening News,* Aug. 1, 1914.
5. *Ibid.,* Aug. 3, 1914.
6. Salt Lake *Tribune,* Aug. 30, 1914.
7. *Solidarity,* Dec. 12, 1914. This was the Eighth Edition of the Song Book. Joe Hill sent along a few suggestions from prison to improve the edition, but they arrived too late to be included. "Will keep them on file for a later edition," commented the editor of *Solidarity* (Dec. 19, 1914).

The leaflet inserted in the Song Books opened: "The Masters of the West Have Selected another active worker in the struggle as a victim in hopes of staying the tide of organization and demands for better conditions that threatens to engulf sacred profits." It then briefly told the story of the shooting of J. G. Morrison and the "circumstantial" evidence used to convict Joe Hill. "Nothing has been proven against him except that he belonged to the I.W.W., which seems sufficient. His attorneys, Scott & McDougall, write, 'The main thing which the state has against Hill is that he is an I.W.W. and *therefore sure to be guilty.'* Such is the case against Hill." (Copy of leaflet in *WSC.*)

8. *Solidarity,* Jan. 9, 1915; *The Herald,* Dec. 26, 1914. *The Herald,* a British labor paper, reported that at the meeting, "Fellow worker Parry showed how the Utah Construction Company lost a strike organized by the I.W.W., and singled out Joe Hill as one of the victims. Ted Fraser gave a number of personal reminiscences of Hill, showing how he organized the workers in the railroad camps, and suffered in the wage-slaves' battle." (Dec. 22, 1914. Copy in British Museum.)

9. Letter and resolution, Jan. 2, 1915, in File No. 174417, Justice Records, Department of Justice, National Archives.

10. Elizabeth Gurley Flynn, *I Speak My Own Piece,* New York, 1955, pp. 179–80; interview with Miss Flynn, New York City, Feb. 10, 1964. Hill's first letter to Miss Flynn, dated Jan. 18, 1915, read: "I want to thank you for what you have done for me and for the interest you have been taking in my welfare, but on the square I'll tell you that all this notoriety stuff is making me dizzy in the head and I am afraid I'm getting more glory than I really am entitled to. I put in most of the later years among the wharfrats on the Pacific coast and I am not there with the lime light stuff at all." (Original in possession of Elizabeth Gurley Flynn.)

11. Stavis, *op. cit.*, p. 46.

12. Morris, *op. cit.*, p. 82.

13. Deseret *Evening News*, Sept. 2, 1914; Salt Lake *Tribune*, Sept. 2, 1914.

14. In the Supreme Court of the State of Utah, *Plaintiff and Respondent vs. Joseph Hillstrom, Appellant and Defendant, Appellant's Brief, Appeal From the Third Judicial District Court of Salt Lake County*, Utah, 56pp. Copy in File 2573, "Joseph Hillstrom," Woodrow Wilson Papers, Library of Congress. Hereinafter cited as *WWP*.

15. "Judge O. N. Hilton in the Joe Hill Case," *International Socialist Review*, vol. XVI, Sept. 1915, pp. 171–72.

16. *Solidarity*, June 12, 1915; "The Last Letters of Joe Hill," *op. cit.*, p. 53.

17. State v. Hillstrom, 46 Utah, 346.

18. *Ibid.*, 349.

19. *Ibid.*, 348.

20. *Ibid.*, 355–56.

21. *Ibid.*, 356.

22. *Ibid.*, 349.

23. *Ibid.*, 357.

24. *Ibid.*, 359. Emphasis mine, *P.S.F.*

25. *Ibid.*, 366. Morris is critical of Hilton and Christensen for not having realized that Judge Ritchie had actually appointed McDougall and Scott as full-fledged counsel rather than as supplementary *amicae curiae* "who merely assist regular counsel or the court. Hilton's and Christensen's only grievance was that the appointment had been made contrary to the objections of Hill, that it was therefore legal error, and that it worked to the detriment of the accused." (*op. cit.*, p. 77.) His point is well taken.

26. State v. Karas, 43 Utah, 506, 136, P. 788 (1913). Emphasis mine, *P.S.F.*

27. State v. Hillstrom, 46 Utah, 376–77.

28. Deseret *Evening News*, June 2–3, Sept. 25, 1915; Modesto, *op. cit.*, p. 45.

29. Deseret *Evening News*, Aug. 2, 1915.

30. *Solidarity*, July 24, 1915.

31. Original in possession of Elizabeth Gurley Flynn.

32. *Solidarity*, July 31, 1915.

33. Stavis, *op. cit.*, pp. 52–54.

34. Letter dated, State Prison, Aug. 15, 1915, and published in Salt Lake *Telegram*, Aug. 22, 1915.

35. Stavis, *op. cit.*, pp. 56–57. Joe Hill finally acquiesced in the I.W.W.'s decision to continue the fight. "I didn't think I'd be worth any more money," he wrote to Sam Murray on Aug. 12, "but I guess the organization thinks otherwise and majority rule goes with me." ("The Last Letters of Joe Hill, *op. cit.*, p. 53.)

36. *American Socialist*, Aug. 28, 1915. Debs wrote of the man facing execution: "Joe Hill is of a poetic temperament and is the author of songs of labor of genuine merit; he is of a tender, sympathetic and generous nature and utterly incapable of committing the crime charged against him." In his letter to Elizabeth Gurley Flynn, Debs wrote: "As the A(merican) S(ocialist) is the party paper and all socialist papers receive it in exchange it is quite probable that a number of them will copy this article. . . . I will gladly do anything more I can and I shall find other ways of getting publicity and reaching

the people." (Eugene V. Debs to Dear Comrade Flynn, Aug. 20, 1915, original in possession of Miss Flynn.)

37. Frank P. Walsh to Elizabeth Gurley Flynn, Aug. 20, 1915, original in possession of Miss Flynn; copy in Frank P. Walsh Papers, New York Public Library.

38. Leaflet in *LC*, gift of Ralph Chaplin, May 1, 1936.

39. Salt Lake *Herald-Republican*, Aug. 13, 1915.

40. Stavis, *op. cit.*, pp. 59–60.

41. Salt Lake *Telegram*, Sept. 14, 1915.

42. Seattle *Times*, Sept. 11, 1915. The meeting was presided over by H. M. Wells, president of the Central Labor Council; Ed T. Levi, business agent of the Waiters' Union, spoke for the A.F. of L. unions; Martin F. Flyzik, state district president of the U.M.W., spoke for the Socialist Party, and James P. Thompson for the I.W.W. (Seattle *Times*, Sept. 11, 1915.)

43. *Solidarity*, Aug. 14, 21, 28, 1915.

44. Deseret *Evening News*, Sept. 4, 1915. The letter was signed by C. Reeve, national organizer, I.W.W.; Boilermakers' Union; Amalgamated Society of Carpenters, Tramway & Railway Employees; Surface Workers' Union; Australia Workers' Union; Post & Telegraph Union of Australia; Australian Shop Assistants' Union, and Federated Mine Workers of Australia. Although the Deseret *Evening News* carried the names of these leading Australian unions along with the Australian I.W.W., editorially it referred to the news as "That I.W.W. Boycott." Since "the I.W.W. tribe" never figured much as "buyers in the markets," American manufacturers were advised to ignore the news from Australia. (*Ibid.*, Sept. 6, 1915.)

45. Salt Lake *Telegram*, Sept. 18, 1915.

46. *The New York Times*, Sept. 20, 1915.

47. Deseret *Evening News*, Sept. 19, 1915. Commenting on what he called "these alleged threats," Judge Hilton wrote that "every indication is that they [the Salt Lake City Officials] are writing these letters themselves, addressed to themselves, or procuring it to be done." (O. N. Hilton to W. A. K. Ekengren, Swedish Minister to the United States, Oct. 22, 1915, Archives of the Royal Ministry of Foreign Affairs, Stockholm, Sweden. Hereinafter cited as *AMFA*.)

Morris believes that if threatening letters had not been sent to Salt Lake City officials with promises of retaliation, "Hill possibly would have won the day" (*op. cit.*, p. 83). But this is a mere supposition, based on no real evidence, and the chances that Hill would have emerged victorious from the Pardon Board hearings were so slight that there is nothing to justify Morris's conclusion.

48. *The New York Times*, Sept. 20, 1915; Deseret *Evening News*, Sept. 24, 1915.

49. Deseret *Evening News*, Sept. 25, 1915.

50. Salt Lake *Tribune*, Sept. 19, 1915; Deseret *Evening News*, Sept. 20, 1915. Hilton was not entirely accurate in his point about the Frank case. It is true that Frank had a weak defense (although it is difficult to see how any defense, however excellent, could have saved him from the death penalty in the biased atmosphere of Atlanta), but Governor Slaton did not refer to the poor defense in commuting the sentence to life imprisonment. He referred

to the facts in the case and insisted that they proved that Frank could not have committed the murder he was charged with.

51. Deseret *Evening News,* Sept. 20, 1915.

52. *Ibid.,* Sept. 25, 1915.

53. *Ibid.*

54. Salt Lake *Telegram,* Sept. 19, 20, 1915.

55. Deseret *Evening News,* Sept. 20, 1915; Salt Lake *Tribune,* Sept. 20, 1915.

56. Salt Lake *Telegram,* Sept. 20, 1915. Haywood wired Senator Lane of Oregon on Sept. 23: "Kindly interview Swedish Minister. Have him ask Secretary of State Lansing to delay execution pending investigation of Joseph Hillstrom a Swedish subject sentenced to be shot October First at Salt Lake City." This telegram was forwarded to the State Department. (Department of State File 311.582H55/original thru 35, National Archives. Hereinafter cited as State Department File, *NA.*) Three days earlier, Haywood had wired Ekengren: "Will you request Secy State Lansing to delay execution pending investigation" (Sept. 20, 1915, *AMFA*).

57. Virginia S. Stephens to W. A. F. Ekengren, Sept. 21, 1915, *AMFA.* *See* also Deseret *Evening News,* Sept. 28, 1915. According to one Swedish writer who has made a study of the case in Sweden, "not once during the campaign for Joe Hill's life does there seem to have been much interest in the Swedish labor press. During the very last weeks before the execution, short articles did appear in a couple of papers with the smallest circulation. However, no labor politician or labor journalist seems to have paid the least attention to the question of Joseph Hillstrom's origin." (John Takman, "Joe Hill's Sister: An Interview," *op. cit.,* p. 27.) The absence of cables or letters from Swedish trade unions or other labor organizations in the State Department Archives, the Woodrow Wilson Papers or the Archives of the Royal Ministry of Foreign Affairs in Stockholm, would seem to confirm this conclusion. Moreover, in his book on Joe Hill, the Swedish writer Ture Nerman does not mention any protests by the Swedish labor press (Ture Nerman, *Arbetarsångaren Joe Hill: Mördare Eller Martyr?,* Stockholm, 1951).

58. Deseret *Evening News,* Sept. 23, 1915.

59. Ekengren to Carlson, Sept. 22, 1915, *AMFA.*

60. Tom Mooney, Secretary, International Workers Defense League, San Francisco, to Ekengren, Sept. 26, 1915, *AMFA.*

61. Carlson to Ekengren, Sept. 22, 1915, *AMFA.*

62. On Sept. 24, Carlson wired Ekengren indignantly protesting the fact that "members of a Swedish Socialist organization" and Virginia S. Stephens and Sigrid Bolin "object to my opinion and insist that Hillstrom did not have a fair trial. The Governor of the state has recd hundreds of letters in Hillstrom behalf." (Carlson to Ekengren, Sept. 24, 1915, *AMFA.*)

63. There are scores of such letters in the Archives of the Royal Ministry of Foreign Affairs, Stockholm, Sweden.

64. Jerome B. Sabath to Ekengren, Sept. 22, 1915, *AMFA.* This was a copy of a memorandum the Association had sent Robert A. Lansing, Secretary of State, on Sept. 15, 1915. It was accompanied by an appeal that Lansing "prevent this execution so that his [Hill's] innocence may be proven." (State Department File, *NA.*)

65. Frank B. Scott to Ekengren, Sept. 24, 1915, *AMFA.*

66. Ekengren to Mrs. J. Sargent Cram, Sept. 24, 1915, *AMFA.* Mrs. Cram, sister-in-law of Gifford Pinchot, was the wife of a member of the New York Public Service Commission who was a power in the Democratic Party. She had been informed of the case by Elizabeth Gurley Flynn and immediately became active in the defense campaign (Flynn, *op. cit.,* p. 181). On Sept. 22, Mrs. Cram wired Ekengren: "I wish Joseph Hillstrom an innocent Swedish subject condemned to death reprieved. Please use your influence with the President of the United States and the Governor of Utah to obtain justice for him" (*AMFA*).

67. Ekengren to Carlson, Sept. 24, 1915; Ekengren to Tom Mooney, Sept. 26, 1915, *AMFA.*

68. Ekengren to Polk, Sept. 25, 1915; Polk to Gov. Spry, Sept. 25, 1915, State Department File, *NA. See also* Deseret *Evening News,* Sept. 27, 1915.

69. Spry to Polk, Sept. 26, 1915, State Department File, *NA.*

70. Deseret *Evening News,* Sept. 29, 1915. "Unless the state department asks for a reprieve or something new concerning the case is brought to light before Friday morning (Oct. 1)," the Deseret *Evening News* reported, "Joseph Hillstrom will be shot to death at that time, officials say. If the state department should ask for a reprieve, in courtesy to the national government, it would probably be granted. It is not now expected by state officials, however, that such a request will be made by the secretary of state."

71. Polk to W. E. Germax, Sept. 28, 1915; Polk to Senator Lane, Sept. 28, 1915, State Department File, *NA.*

72. Ekengren to Polk, Sept. 28, 1915, State Department File, *NA.*

73. Jane Addams to Ekengren, Sept. 28, 1915, enclosing letter of William L. Chenery; William L. Chenery to Ekengren, Sept. 25, 1915, *AMFA.*

74. Theodora Pollok to Ekengren, Sept. 25, Oct. 2, 1915, *AMFA.*

75. Jensen, "The Legend of Joe Hill," *op. cit.,* p. 363.

76. Ekengren to Polk, Sept. 29, 1915, enclosing message to Gov. Spry, State Department File, *NA:* Deseret *Evening News,* Sept. 30, 1915.

77. Deseret *Evening News,* Sept. 29, 1915.

78. *Ibid.,* Sept. 30, 1915.

79. Ekengren to Spry, Sept. 30, 1915, *AMFA.*

80. Spry to Ekengren, Sept. 27, 1915, *AMFA.*

81. Carlson to Ekengren, Sept. 28, 1915, *AMFA.*

82. Ekengren to Jos. Hillstrom, Sept. 30, 1915, *AMFA.*

83. Ekengren to Spry, Sept. 30, 1915, *AMFA.*

84. Ekengren to Mrs. J. Sargent Cram, Sept. 30, 1915; Ekengren to Jane Addams, Sept. 30, 1915, *AMFA.*

85. Deseret *Evening News,* Sept. 30, 1915.

86. The original in Swedish was published in the magazine *Revolt.* There is a copy in the Labadie Collection.

87. Deseret *Evening News,* Oct. 1, 1915; *Solidarity,* Oct. 9, 1915. *Solidarity* published the letter under the headline: "All the World May Say: *Here Is A Man.*" One might also say that Joe Hill's letter is a classic example of Wobbly humor.

88. Scott to Tumulty, Sept. 29, 1915, State Department File, *NA;* Deseret *Evening News,* Sept. 30, 1915. Scott followed up the wire with a letter to

Tumulty on Oct. 1, 1915, in which he observed: "It may not be possible to produce any evidence to prove Hillstrom's innocence, but of course he should never have been found guilty under the evidence." He added, however, that "Hillstrom himself, by acting the same way he is acting now, prejudiced the jury against him so they proved him guilty regardless of whether there was evidence or not." (State Department File, *NA*.)

89. O. N. Hilton to Tumulty, Sept. 29, 1915, State Department File, *NA*.

90. Mrs. J. Sargent Cram to Ekengren, Sept. 29, 1915, *AMFA*.

91. Ekengren to Wilson, Sept. 29, 30, 1915, *AMFA* and *WWP*.

92. Deseret *Evening News*, Sept. 30, 1915.

93. *Solidarity*, Oct. 9, 1915.

94. Salt Lake *Tribune*, Oct. 2, 1915.

95. *Solidarity*, Oct. 9, 1915.

96. Modesto, *op. cit.*, p. 50.

97. Joseph Hillstrom to Ekengren, Oct. 1, 1915, *AMFA*: Deseret *Evening News*, Oct. 2, 4, 1915.

98. Deseret *Evening News*, Sept. 28, 1915; Morris, *op. cit.*, p. 100. Soren X. Christensen informed Ekengren that Hill's statement had been given to him by the prisoner, "but under the rules of the penitentiary it must be submitted to the warden first. I have been unable to get it back since. Understand that the pardon board has it. Expect to get it and have it published." (Christensen to Ekengren, Oct. 1, 1915, *AMFA*.)

99. Deseret *Evening News*, Oct. 4, 1915; *Solidarity*, Oct. 16, 1915.

100. Ekengren to Jerome B. Sabath, Oct. 11, 1915, *AMFA*.

101. Salt Lake *Tribune* to Ekengren, Sept. 30, 1915; Frank K. Polk to Ekengren, Oct. 1, 1915; Ekengren to J. Baer Reinhardt, Oct. 8, 1915; Ekengren to Henry G. Gray, Oct. 8, 1915, *AMFA*.

102. Hilton to Ekengren, Oct. 13, 1915, *AMFA*.

103. Ekengren to Mrs. J. Sargent Cram, Oct. 14, 1915, *AMFA*.

104. Both Hilton's draft and Ekengren's letter to Wilson, Oct. 13, 1915, are in *AMFA*. Ekengren's letter is also in *WWP*.

105. Haywood to Ekengren, Oct. 13, 1915, *AMFA*.

106. Wilson to Ekengren, Oct. 16, 1915, *AMFA*.

107. Salt Lake *Tribune*, Oct. 15, 1915; Deseret *Evening News*, Oct. 16, 1915.

108. Deseret *Evening News*, Oct. 16, 1915.

109. Salt Lake *Tribune*, Oct. 17, 1915; Deseret *Evening News*, Oct. 18, 1915. D. A. Leatherwood told the Board of Pardons that it was impossible for Ekengren to have read "the stenographic records of the proceedings before the lower court" since there were only two copies of the Transcript, both of which were locked in a safe in his office (Deseret *Evening News*, Oct. 18, 1915). However, Judge Hilton had a copy of the Transcript and had brought it with him when he travelled to Washington at his own expense to discuss the case with Minister Ekengren. "He seems to be wholly convinced that Joe is being railroaded to his death," Hilton wrote to Elizabeth Gurley Flynn, pointing out that the Swedish Minister had read the Transcript (*Solidarity*, Oct. 16, 1915). Before he obtained a copy of the Transcript from Hilton, Ekengren had written to Judge Ritchie and asked for a complete record of the testimony before the court. The request was turned down (Deseret *Evening News*, Oct. 8, 1915).

110. Deseret *Evening News*, Oct. 18, 1915.

111. Frank E. Lindquist to Ekengren, Oct. 17, 1915, *AMFA;* Deseret *Evening News,* Oct. 20, 1915; Hilton to Ekengren, Oct. 19, 1915, *AMFA.*

112. Ekengren to Royal Foreign Office, Oct. 6, 1915; Swedish Minister to Ekengren (Oct. 8) 1915, *AMFA.* In Swedish.

113. Ekengren to Marcel A. Viti, Oct. 26, 1915; Isaac B. Reinhardt to Ekengren, Oct. 30, 1915; Ekengren to Waldeemar Van Cott, Oct. 25, 1915; Waldeemar Van Cott to Ekengren, Nov. 1, 1915, *AMFA.*

114. Hilton to Ekengren, Oct. 30, 1915, *AMFA.*

115. Ekengren to Hilton, Oct. 26, 1915; Ekengren to Pierce, Critchlow and Barrette, Nov. 3, 6, 1915; Pierce, Critchlow and Barrette to Ekengren, Nov. 6, 1915, *AMFA.*

116. Pierce, Critchlow and Barrette to Ekengren, Nov. 4, 6, 1915, *AMFA.* The idea had been suggested on Sept. 29 by E. D. McDougall who noted that "Utah laws do not permit execution of insane people" (McDougall to Ekengren, Sept. 29, 1915, *AMFA*).

117. Pierce, Critchlow and Barrette to Ekengren, Nov. 10, 1915; Ekengren to Marcel A. Viti, Nov. 18, 1915, *AMFA.*

118. Joseph Hillstrom to Ekengren, Nov. 12, 1915, *AMFA.*

119. Hilton to Ekengren, Oct. 22, 1915, enclosing letter from Buffalo, N.Y.; Ekengren to Chief of Police, Salt Lake City, Oct. 26, 1915; Ekengren to Chief of Police, Buffalo, N.Y., Nov. 6, 1915, *AMFA.* The letter was first sent to Elizabeth Gurley Flynn who forwarded it to Judge Hilton. (Interview with Elizabeth Gurley Flynn, New York City, Jan. 30, 1964. *See also* Ekengren to Chief of Police, Buffalo, N.Y., Nov. 6, 1915, *AMFA.*)

120. Hilton to Joe Hillstrom, Oct. 24, 1915, *AMFA.*

121. Hilton to Isaac B. Reinhardt, copy in Hilton to Ekengren, Oct. 30, 1915, *AMFA.*

122. Copy of petition in *AMFA.* Many of these petitions were forwarded to Spry by the National Association for the Abolition of Capital Punishment (Jerome B. Sabath to Ekengren, Nov. 17–15, *AMFA*).

123. There are scores of such letters dated late October and early November 1915, many in Swedish, in the Archives of the Royal Foreign Minister, Stockholm, Sweden. A typical message read: "We the Scandinavian Viking Society of Edmonton Alberta Canada have held a meeting and investigated the case of Joseph Hillstrom and declare that he is fully innocent and also that his trial was a very unfair one. We apply to you to protest against the execution of said Joseph Hillstrom and ask that a new trial be granted" (Nov. 17, 1915, *AMFA*). After describing himself as one who "believe[s] in the absolute innocence of the man," Timothy Walsh, financial editor of the New York *World,* wrote: "I am glad to see that the Swedes have taken the matter up and hope something good comes of their efforts" (Walsh to Ekengren, Nov. 9, 1915, *AMFA*). On Nov. 7, 1915, the New York *World* carried a long article on the case which included an interview with Elizabeth Gurley Flynn indicating the reasons why she believed Joe Hill innocent. The article was entitled, "Elizabeth Flynn in Fight to Save I.W.W. Murderer."

124. All of these letters are in State Department File, *NA.*

125. Central Labor Council, Seattle, Halet M. Wells, President, to Wilson, Nov. 14, 1915, State Department File, *NA.* The letter added: "If you would safeguard the best interests of this nation of ours . . . we implore you at this moment when 'National Preparedness' is the cry heard above all other

things, to remember that the first essential to the success of any such program is the confidence and support of the workers and this confidence cannot be established or maintained by the legalized murder of the workers nor as long as they conscientiously believe that this condition exists." It is doubtful if Joe Hill would have approved of this type of plea in his behalf. He was vigorously opposed to preparations for war. On Sept. 9, 1915, he wrote to his friend Sam Murray: "Millions of men are employed at making ships and others are hired to sink them. Scientific management, eh, wot?" ("The Last Letters of Joe Hill," *op. cit.,* p. 54.)

126. Rave Taylor, President, to Wilson, Nov. 4, 1915, State Department File, *NA.*

127. Signed by Harold L. Lloyd, Harry Feinberg, and James P. Thompson, Nov. 14, 1915, State Department File, *NA.*

128. All copies of the petition are in State Department File, *NA.* The petitions were distributed by John Sandgren, Swedish Secretary of the Joe Hill Defense Committee, with the request that they be mailed to President Wilson, Governor Spry, local mayors, and the press. They were forwarded to the Department of Justice, and Alvery A. Adel, wrote to all who were listed as signers:

"The Department desire to express its disapproval of the intemperate language contained in the next to last paragraph of the resolution which bears your signature, and to direct attention to the consequences possibly attending the use of such language." (The paragraph referred to is the one which begins, "Resolved, That in such a case. . . .") At first Adel had added, "particularly naturalized citizens who may become naturalized," but he must have reconsidered the wisdom of this threat, and it is crossed out in the original draft of the letter. (Alvery A. Adel to Nils Olsen and others, Dec. 2, 1915, State Department File, *NA.*)

129. All of these letters are in State Department File, *NA* and *WWP.* I. Amter, who was later a leader of the Communist Party, wrote from Corona, Long Island, on Oct. 20, 1915: "Joe Hillstrom is a fighter for the downtrodden. . . . Joe Hillstrom is a valiant fighter for the working class, and I add my voice to the many that have been and will be raised in protest against his execution and in demand for the new trial that he is entitled to and has asked for" (State Department File, *NA*).

130. Bernard Kyler to Wilson, Oct. 29, 1915, State Department File, *NA.*

131. Flynn, *op. cit.,* pp. 181–82.

132. Helen Keller to Wilson, Nov. 16, 1915; Wilson to Helen Keller, Nov. 17, 1915, *WWP.*

133. Deseret *Evening News,* Oct. 19, 20, 22, 29; Nov. 13, 14, 1915.

134. *Ibid.,* Oct. 19, 1915. An indication of the hysteria that swept the West over the Joe Hill case is revealed in a report of an undercover investigator for Governor Hiram Johnson of California. He wrote, without offering the slightest evidence, that he had learned of a "plan on foot [by the I.W.W. in San Francisco] to start something there [Salt Lake City] at the time of Hillstrom's execution in the way of a 'social revolution.' " (E. Clemens Horst Investigation, Report of Ethel Loar for Nov. 2 & 3, 1915, at Sacramento and San Francisco, Hiram Johnson Papers, University of California Library, Berkeley.)

135. Deseret *Evening News,* Nov. 8, 1915; Morris, *op. cit.,* pp. 109–10.

136. Deseret *Evening News,* Nov. 17, 1915.

137. *Proceedings,* A.F. of L. Convention, 1915, pp. 103–05, 167–69. A number of A.F. of L. officials in Salt Lake City, however, were infuriated by the resolution and claimed that it did not reflect their opinion (Deseret *Evening News,* Nov. 17, 19, 1915).

138. Deseret *Evening News,* Nov. 17, 1915; Gompers to Wilson, Nov. 16, 1915, *WWP;* Gompers to Ekengren, Nov. 16, 1915, *AMFA.* On Nov. 2, the Salt Lake *Telegram* carried an interview with Gompers who was on his way to the San Francisco convention. Asked if he had heard about the Hill case, Gompers replied: "Yes, yes, I have heard and read about the case of Hillstrom and I hope that the Governor of your state, in the bigness of his heart, will extend clemency to this man until the condition of his case can be further investigated." On the other hand, the *American Federationist,* which Gompers edited, did not have a single item about the case before the convention.

139. Wilson to Spry, Nov. 17, 1915; Wilson to Gompers, Nov. 17, 1915, *WWP;* Deseret *Evening News,* Nov. 17, 18, 1915.

140. Jerome B. Sabath to Ekengren, Nov. 17–15, *AMFA.*

141. Spry to Wilson, Nov. 18, 1915, *WWP;* Deseret *Evening News,* Nov. 18, 1915.

142. Editorial, Nov. 18, 1915, clipping enclosed in William Glassman to Wilson, Nov. 20, 1915, *WWP.*

143. Salt Lake *Herald-Republican,* Nov. 18, 1915; Salt Lake *Tribune,* Nov. 18, 1915; Deseret *Evening News,* Nov. 18, 1915. In the presidential election of 1916, where Wilson ran against Charles Evans Hughes, the Republican Party of Utah issued a pamphlet reprinting the correspondence between President Wilson and Governor Spry. The front page of the pamphlet carried the following:

"I.W.W.

"In the Case of Georgia President Wilson refused to interfere with the process of the Courts. He told 2,000,000 petitioners in behalf of Leo M. Frank that as President of the United States he could not interfere with the operation of justice in a sovereign state.

"In the Case of Utah President Wilson interfered, not once, but a second time and insulted the integrity of Utah Justice. . . . Why did he honor Georgia and dishonor Utah?"

The *Industrial Worker,* western organ of the I.W.W., reprinted the first page of the pamphlet, but perhaps fearing that Wobblies might be induced to vote for Wilson out of gratitude for his role in the Joe Hill case, swiftly added: "President Wilson is not entitled to any credit for his stand on this matter as he was forced into action by the representative of Sweden in the United States. The workers can expect nothing from politicians, but politicians can expect much from an awakened working class, and all of it disagreeable." (Nov. 4, 1916.)

Wilson does not appear to have been disturbed by these attacks upon him for the role he played in the Joe Hill case. Thus he penciled on an attack by Senator Reed Smoot of Utah: "Dear Tumulty: I would be obliged if you would say that I do not think any attention ought to be paid to these attacks. They answer themselves." (Attached to clipping from Salt Lake *Tribune,* Oct. 12, 1916, in *WWP.*)

144. Deseret *Evening News,* Nov. 18, 1915. Probably the suit was the

"good" one in which Hill wished to be buried, and was a gift from the
I.W.W. Even though the whole story was ludicrous, it was taken seriously by
the Salt Lake City press and undoubtedly convinced a number of people that
Hill was certainly guilty.

145. Salt Lake *Herald-Republican,* Nov. 18, 1915. The Deseret *Evening
News* did not publish the text of the will, merely reporting: "Hillstrom wrote
verses in place of a will" (Nov. 19, 1915).

146. Phil Engle, member of the delegation, in *Industrial Worker,* Jan. 20,
1917.

147. *International Socialist Review,* vol. XVI, Dec. 1915, pp. 328–31.

148. Philip S. Foner, editor, *The Letters of Joe Hill,* New York, 1965, p. 42.
The Deseret *Evening News* described the song as "of a sentimental nature
and refers to the breaking up of families by war" (Nov. 19, 1915).

CHAPTER V

1. International News Service Report of Execution of Joe Hill, Salt Lake,
Utah, Nov. 19, 1915, copy in *WSC.*

2. Hilton to Ekengren, Nov. 19, 1915, *AMFA;* Deseret *Evening News,* Nov.
19, 20, 1915. An attempt was made to get President Wilson to intervene once
again on the basis of Busky's affidavit. Thomas Whitehead of Seattle wired
Wilson on Nov. 19: "Man here makes affidavit he was with Joseph Hillstrom
from two until ten P.M. on day of Morrison murder. Request stay of execution
to allow introduction of this new evidence." On the telegram, there is the
note: "Referred to chf clk Davis personally without comment." (*WWP.*) It
is not clear why the Defense Committee or the I.W.W. did not pursue the
Busky matter even after Hill's execution. Publication of a detailed account of
the time he spent with Hill on the night of the murder, together with a
careful effort to authenticate his statement, would have made a great impression on the American people.

3. Salt Lake *Telegram,* Nov. 21, 22, 1915.

4. Deseret *Evening News,* Nov. 26, 1915. Hilton informed Ekengren that
"it would greatly please everybody" if he could attend the services, but the
Minister replied that "highly important business" prevented him from leaving
Washington. (Hilton to Ekengren, Nov. 21, 1915, and undated telegram,
Ekengren to Hilton, *AMFA.*)

5. Deseret *Evening News,* Nov. 26, 1915; Ralph Chaplin, "Joe Hill's
Funeral," *International Socialist Review,* vol. XVI, Jan. 1916, pp. 400–05;
Solidarity, Dec. 4, 1915.

6. *Industrial Worker,* Dec. 2, 1916.

CHAPTER VI

1. Hilton to Ekengren, Nov. 19, 1915; Ekengren to Hilton, Nov. 27, 1915,
AMFA. In his letter, Hilton wrote: "I have felt and suffered over this matter
more than I can possibly express to you as I was drawn closely to Hillstrom
by peculiar ties seemingly stronger than those which usually obtain in the
relation of Attorney and Client, and I have always and still do believe
implicitly in his innocence. That I have not been recompensed in dollars is of

no possible moment, and while I shall expect nothing in this respect, from any source, there is one thing I would highly appreciate and prize more than money, and that is some small insignia from your government, that I have done all I could to safeguard and protect the liberty and life of one of its subjects." Ekengren assured the Denver attorney that his "selfsacrificing and untiring work in connection with this case" would not go unnoticed by the Swedish government, and that "my Government in consideration of your praiseworthy efforts to obtain justice for my unfortunate countryman will in some way or other show its appreciation for what you have done in this matter." (Hilton to Ekengren, Nov. 19, 1915; Ekengren to Hilton, Nov. 27, 1915, *AMFA.*) There is nothing to indicate that the Swedish government ever did act in this matter.

2. Ekengren to Han Excellens Herr Ministern för Utrikes Ärendena, June 18, 1916, *AMFA.* In Swedish.

3. Deseret *Evening News,* Nov. 19, 1915.

4. *Ibid.,* Nov. 13, 1915, and Elizabeth Gurley Flynn, in *The Worker,* Nov. 14, 1934.

5. Salt Lake *Tribune,* Dec. 22, 1915.

6. Hilton to Ekengren, Dec. 21, 1915, *AMFA.*

7. Hilton to Ekengren, Dec. 25, 1915, *AMFA.*

8. In re Hilton, 158 Pacific Reporter, 691–93. Hilton was readmitted to the bar on September 14, 1923.

9. Reprinted in Deseret *Evening News,* Nov. 30, 1915.

10. Detroit *Labor News,* Nov. 26, 1915.

11. Jim Larkin, "Murder Most Foul," *International Socialist Review,* vol. XVI, Dec. 1915, p. 330.

12. Emma Goldman to Agnes Ingles, Nov. 23, 1915; *LC;* Morris, *op. cit.,* p. 121.

13. Ralph Chaplin, "Joe Hill," *International Socialist Review,* vol. XVI, Dec. 1915, p. 325.

14. *The New York Times,* Nov. 20, 1915.

15. Deseret *Evening News,* Nov. 19, 1915.

CHAPTER VII

1. *The Utah Survey,* April, 1915, p. 16.

2. J. Kenneth Davis, "Mormonism and the Closed Shop," *Labor History,* vol. III, Spring, 1962, pp. 172–74.

3. Hilton to Joe Hill, July 19, 1915, original in possession of Elizabeth Gurley Flynn.

4. Jensen, "The Legend of Joe Hill," *op. cit.,* p. 359.

5. Salt Lake *Telegram,* Sept. 20, 1915. "Hillstrom," Christensen added, "believes himself a martyr. He feels that he is giving his life to advance the spirit of fair trials in Utah." One is privileged, like some writers, to sneer at this, but there is little doubt that Joe Hill felt this sincerely, even though he did write to Elizabeth Gurley Flynn: "I have absolutely no desire to be one of them what-ye-call-em martyrs." (Philip S. Foner, editor, *The Letters of Joe Hill,* p. 24.)

In his unpublished study, "The Case of Joe Hill," James O. Morris, after a careful examination of all the evidence, reaches the conclusion "that Hill was not treated fairly in the courts or before the Pardon Board"; that "Hill was not incriminated in the least in the witnesses' descriptions of the man they saw near the store before or after the murder"; that "the evidence did not find Hill guilty beyond a reasonable doubt," and that the fact that he was active in the I.W.W., more than anything else, led to his execution. (*op. cit.,* pp. 122–27.) But he also concludes that Joe Hill was probably the man who shot Morrison and his son, and reaches this conclusion on the basis of a most tortured type of reasoning. He bases this not on the evidence produced against Hill by any of the witnesses, but on what they did not say, and on the supposition that the bullet which was supposed to have entered and passed through Hill's body lodged in the ceiling and therefore was never found in the grocery store. (*op. cit.,* pp. 129–31.) In reaching this conclusion, Morris entirely abandons a scientific approach and engages in sheer speculation, an odd way in which to judge the innocence or guilt of a person executed for a crime he did not commit.

6. International News Service Report of Execution of Joe Hill, Salt Lake, Utah, Nov. 19, 1915, copy in *WSC.*